Yo
Life Style
Diet

# Your Life Style Diet

ISABEL SKYPALA
AND
DIANA HUTCHINSON

CHAPMANS

Chapmans Publishers Ltd
141–143 Drury Lane
London WC2B 5TB

British Library Cataloguing in Publication Data

Skypala, Isabel
Your life style diet.
I. Title   II. Hutchinson, Diana
613.25

ISBN 1-85592-562-1

First published by Chapmans 1991
Copyright © Isabel Skypala and Diana Hutchinson 1991

Photoset by Rowland Phototypesetting Ltd,
Bury St Edmunds, Suffolk
Printed and bound in Great Britain by
Clays Ltd, St Ives plc

Designed by Judy Linard
Illustrations by Kate Thompson

# Contents

# Charts and Tables

# Introduction

At any one time a quarter of all women in the UK are trying to lose weight. Although more men than women are overweight, most dieters are women. Thousands go on a new diet each year in the hopes of looking slim for their holidays or some special occasion. Almost every diet will work if you stick to it. The sad truth is many successful dieters put back on all the weight they spent precious months trying to lose. Those who have lost a lot of weight quickly can end up regaining it just as fast, often weighing more than before they started dieting.

So thousands of women are treading a cycle of deprivation, starvation and disappointment in the long term. As one colleague told us: 'I have been losing the same seven pounds for the last ten years.' Is all this dieting really necessary? Dawn French is needed and valued in this world just as much as Julia Roberts. Do we need to lose so much weight? Are we losing weight for the sake of our health? Or do we aspire to be on the skinny side of slender out of vanity or to fit in with other people's expectations? Where our bodies are concerned, do we go for the norm or aim for perfection?

As a nation we are becoming taller and heavier, for the good reason that we are better nourished than ever before. Although a third of the adult population need to lose weight, being slightly heavier than your colleagues and friends does not mean you are overweight. Many so-called 'perfect' weight tables give quite low recommendations. Don't let them panic you into serious dieting if you are happy with your body the way it is. You can then get caught in the diet trap and find it hard to escape.

For most people, being a stone overweight will not affect your health. THE PROBLEM IS THAT FOR SOME PEOPLE ONE STONE OVER THE ODDS GRADUALLY BUILDS UP TO TWO. Before they realise it they may be three or four stone heavier than is good for them. Health problems cannot be caused by excess weight alone, but if you are more than two stone overweight, you are more likely to get high blood pressure, varicose veins, a high blood cholesterol level, diabetes and heart disease, as you get older. It is a fact that people who are very overweight cannot expect to live as long as the rest of us.

Most overweight adults put on fat during their late twenties and early thirties. Perhaps they are not so active as they were as teenagers, or maybe they have lost the spare time and inclination to take part in regular sport. As the years go by we need fewer calories but often continue to eat just as much if not more than we need.

A changing life style should be matched by a change in diet. We may be trying to cram in three meals a day when we only have time to eat snacks. We often eat a fattening pub lunch, but still go home to a heavy evening meal with all the family.

The keys to successful weight loss are a well-planned diet and the will to succeed. Many of the people referred for slimming advice to Isabel, a dietitian, are hospital patients with serious health problems. They have the motivation to lose weight because they know it will help their breathing problems or heart condition. They understand why they cannot afford to put it all back on again. Diana has spent many years selecting and editing other people's diets and dealing with slimming queries from readers. She has personally tried out many diets but never found one to suit the unsocial hours and missed meals that are typical of the life style of a working journalist. That is until she met Isabel.

So Isabel really has to get to the bottom of why this particular person is overweight. Once this is established Isabel can design a diet which suits exactly. One thing we have learned is that however powerful their motivation, even if it is a matter of life or death, most people find it difficult to stay slim if a diet is not easy to follow or does not fit in with their life style.

We also take into account what they do for a living. People in different jobs have different levels of activity. For example, as a profession, nurses generally do more physical work than secretaries. A bank clerk will use less energy than a P.T. instructor. A policewoman on the beat consumes more energy than a housewife. It might be better to advise everyone to use more energy by taking more exercise. You could run the last half mile to work, but would you do it each day come rain or shine? How much good would it really do you? It is much easier and more realistic to match the diet to the amount of energy that person would normally use in the course of their daily work. DIETS WHICH DO NOT TAKE INTO ACCOUNT YOUR WAY OF LIFE ARE VERY HIT AND MISS AFFAIRS.

Many slimming diets give rigid guidelines on exactly

what you should eat at every meal. The truth is we generally only eat such food as is readily available to us. Is it realistic to expect people to have time to cook special elaborate diet meals, make up special slimming soups, live on nothing but salads or start every day with a grapefruit and a boiled egg? Whether you eat at home, in a snack bar, at a fast food café or grab a pub lunch THE FOOD ON A SUCCESSFUL DIET MUST FIT IN WITH YOUR LIFE STYLE. You may have to entertain clients, buy your round of cakes for the office or have that Friday drink. A diet that expects you to say, 'Sorry, not me' will not work for long.

Amongst the rich and famous it is fashionable to have your own nutritional 'expert', just as it is smart to use a personal trainer. If you have a major weight problem the services of a dietitian should be available to you through your doctor or local hospital. But for those of you who cannot easily get to see a dietitian, this book is the next best thing.

*Your Life Style Diet* is flexible but not vague. It lets you choose from the kind of food you would normally eat, but calorie counted to be just enough for your daily needs. It will suggest what to choose when the only place open is a fast food café. It advises on the pitfalls of overseas travel, and will even guide you in the sandwich bar, Indian takeaway or chill freeze cabinet in the supermarket.

Using this book is easy. But before you set off, take some time to think about the way you spend your day. Does your work involve a lot of sitting down? Are you working unsocial hours? Do you travel a good deal or are you based at home? It makes all the difference.

Look at the tables on pages 23 and 24 and see what you expect to weigh. This is going to be your *personal* diet, so answer the quiz on page 26. It will help you sort out which is the right way to lose weight for you. It is all based on the amount of energy you expend and the kind of food convenient to you.

That's why there is such a big 'dictionary' of foods. We give the calorie values of fresh foods but also include ready meals you buy from the freezer, in fast food cafés or in bars and restaurants.

You will probably find that you want to carry this book around with you. It will become your personal guide to a slimmer, fitter figure.

# 1 What Makes People Fat?

The first step in *Your Life Style Diet* is understanding why you have put on weight. YOU WILL PUT ON WEIGHT IF YOUR ENERGY BALANCE HAS BEEN UPSET. This happens when the food you eat gives you more energy than you use up. But how much is too much?

The number of calories you need depends on your age, sex and activity. The latest official guidelines, published in 1991, give figures based on our physical activity (both at work and at home) multiplied by our basal metabolic rate (see page 19). They suggest that most women aged between 19 and 49 need around 1,940 calories a day. If you are moderately active at home and work, they allow 2,200 calories a day. Very active women should be aiming for 2,500 calories.

The vast majority trying to slim have no medical reason for their current spare tyre. There is no alibi to hide behind. The body is simply storing unused calories as fat. An inbuilt survival mechanism makes sure any excess energy does not go to waste. Humans did not always enjoy a continuous supply of food. In times of plenty, the best way of storing excess energy was as fat. This could be converted back into energy when they fell on hard times. Today, Western nations have a plentiful supply of food, but our bodies still efficiently store excess calories as fat. SO DON'T HATE YOUR BODY. After all it is only trying to do its job.

Some people are less efficient at storing calories than others. They waste their excess energy by turning it into heat. These are the people who seem to be able to eat anything they like without putting on any weight. Experts think that something known as 'brown fat' is used by the body to help turn extra calories into heat. Thin people may have more brown fat than the rest of us. But the sad truth is many thin people, consciously or unconsciously, tune into the body's need for energy. They eat only what they need to keep their weight stable.

If upsetting your energy balance makes you put on weight, knowing what affects it helps you along the road to controlling your weight. Both food and activity affect our energy balance. But for most of us, food is the more important. It provides us with protein, fat and carbohydrate which give us calories to use for energy. These days we eat about 2,200 calories daily compared to an average of 2,500 calories at the beginning of the 1970s. Before the Second World War, in the days of roast beef and Yorkshire pudding, spotted dick and custard cuisine, people ate even more.

However, there are more overweight people than ever before because we are also far less active than we used to be. Our daily trip to school included a stiff uphill walk of one mile. How many schoolchildren can say that today? People walked or cycled rather than travelled by car. One hundred years ago most of our energy came from starchy carbohydrate foods such as bread and potatoes. They helped sustain us through the long working day. Now our diet is dominated by fatty foods such as meat, cheese and fried foods.

Our parents tried to eat three full meals each day and agonised over their children who missed a meal. Usually the largest intake of calories was at midday, with a lighter tea or supper in the evening. Now because we travel much longer journeys to work, or all the household have different schedules, we meet to eat at night. Many people eat very little during the day, keeping up their energy with sandwiches, chocolate bars and crisps. At night they compound the mischief by eating a large meal quite late and then slump in front of the television. Is it any wonder our average weight as a nation goes up and up?

The way we eat and what we eat affects our energy balance. Many people who are overweight feel quite cheated. They could never be called greedy. They eat sparingly or not at all during the day, consume most of their calories over a social meal at night. They are too busy at work for a proper lunch. They would miss their train if they stopped to eat breakfast. At night they can sit back and feast with a clear conscience. Surely they have saved up all the permitted day's calories for one big meal.

But your body is more intelligent than you give it credit for. Starve it all day, and it simply lowers its metabolic rate so that it can cope on zero calories. Your body's need for energy is at its all time low during the evening and night. Scoff the whole of your calorie allowance in the evening, and you will simply store most of it as fat. You want to keep slim. Your body wants to survive and function.

If this scenario is one you are familiar with, think about why you eat. Is it really because you are hungry? Perhaps you eat because you are bored by your undemanding job. Is the grind of your daily routine or commuter journey driving you to the corner shop or burger bar? Do you join in the afternoon tea session and tuck into cream cakes because everyone else does?

Some jobs mean that many people do not eat regular sit-down meals at all. They eat snacks throughout the day. This is known as grazing. Grazing is not necessarily bad. Eating six small meals or snacks in a day can be as good as three larger meals, so long as the snacks are not too high in calories and eaten at regular times of day. The problem is so many ready-made snacks are appallingly high in calories and fat.

There are overweight people who really do not overindulge and it is hard to see what else they can cut out to lose weight. The reason they are fat is because at some point in their lives they must have eaten more calories than they need. Perhaps it happened at a stressful time in their lives. Some people lose weight during periods of stress or nervous energy. This is not caused by their nervous energy using up more calories, but because they naturally eat very little at such times. Unfortunately it is too often the opposite that is true. At stressful times, sugary drinks and biscuits fly into the hand without us noticing. Or we live off bits and pieces of food and never sit down for a proper meal. You can get through a lot of calories when you do not have a set food routine. Also bits and pieces can be very high in calories.

Perhaps it is not stress but just the opposite, that causes the mysterious weight gain. Everyone loses weight to go on holiday. How many weigh themselves on their return? Lazing around the pool, eating salads drenched in oil and keeping cool with several icecreams daily is the usual recipe for an extra half-stone. Not to mention those happy hour cocktails and free bar nibbles. If you thought a plunge in the pool or walk to the waterfront exercised it off – look at page 21 and think again!

All activities use up some calories. The way your body uses the calories you feed it also affects your energy balance. The amount of energy you need depends on your *basal metabolic rate* (BMR), the rate at which you use calories for your body to function. Most of the calories you eat are used to keep your body ticking over. Someone with a low BMR will therefore need fewer calories than someone with a high BMR.

It is very difficult to change your BMR . . . magically to be able to eat as much as you like without putting on weight. BMR goes up after exercise, but returns to normal soon afterwards. If you exercise regularly over a period of time, your BMR will gradually increase and stay at a higher level. But it will drop again eventually if you stop taking exercise. If you are overweight it can be difficult to do the type of strenuous exercise that would increase your BMR.

Your BMR can be affected by food as well as exercise. This happens in two ways. The digestion of protein, fat and carbohydrate increases your BMR. Protein causes the greatest increase, followed by fat and then carbohydrate. This is known as the thermogenic effect of food. If you eat normally, your BMR will rise by 5 to 10% over twenty-four hours. However most experts feel this is not great enough to justify designing a slimming diet around the thermogenic effect. So although protein does increase your BMR, eating a lot of it to try and lose weight is not a good idea. In any case, high protein foods are often high in calories, e.g. red meat and cheese.

Even if the thermogenic effect of food was helpful to

19

slimmers, the second effect food has on your BMR would cancel out any benefit gained. Cut down on your calories and your body will automatically lower your BMR to save energy. Dieting means you eat less, but need less. Losing weight can therefore take longer than you thought. Crash dieting is very bad news for your BMR since the less you eat the further it falls. Coming off your diet will not immediately raise your BMR. So fall back into those bad old eating habits and instant weight gain will be the result. Constant dieting could lead to a permanently low BMR so TREAT YOUR BODY WITH RESPECT AND MAKE YOUR LIFE STYLE DIET YOUR LAST.

Most of the calories you eat are used up by your BMR. Many people do not realise how few calories are used doing daily activities such as walking, sitting and standing. Only 12% of our calorie intake is used up in this way. Strangely, overweight people use up more energy doing simple things like going to the shops, because they have extra weight to carry around. Unfortunately this advantage is lost because many overweight people do less walking and standing than people of a normal weight, because of the extra effort involved.

Although food intake plus activity both affect energy balance, changing what you eat is much more likely to help you lose weight. However you should try and get as much exercise as possible when you are dieting . . . it helps things along, makes you feel good and keeps your heart and lungs healthy.

# YOUR ACTIVITY CALORIE COUNT

| Activity | No. of calories used/hour | Equivalent food |
| --- | --- | --- |
| Sitting | 15 | 1 portion cabbage |
| Ironing | 59 | 20 grapes |
| Driving a truck | 150 | 2 butter portions |
| Walking | 115 | 1oz cheese |
| Brisk walking | 215 | 3 plain biscuits |
| Gardening | 300 | Slice chocolate cake |
| Dancing | 480 | Large packet tortilla chips |
| Walking up & down 1 flight of stairs | 540 | 1 pork pie |
| Swimming | 600 | 2 cheeseburgers |
| Running | 600 | 2 Mars bars |

# *What should I weigh?*

Tables of suggested weights for heights give you an idea about how much you should weigh, but do not take them as gospel. Two women of the same age and height can both look good at weights which might differ by up to a stone. Never compare yourself to other people. Before you start your diet, take a good look at yourself in the mirror. Try to see yourself as others see you. You may have a larger bottom than you would like, but is dieting going to radically change that? All dieting may do is make you lose weight from your waist and accentuate your bottom even more.

When you diet, you are most likely to lose weight from your tummy, bust, back and upper arms first. It is more difficult to lose weight from hips and thighs, but can be done if you keep dieting and make sure you also keep on the move. Once you have decided that you have excess flab that you can get rid of, then have a look at the charts and see what they say.

The charts used in this book are similar to those used by dietitians and doctors to check your weight. Chart A is based on weights recommended by the Royal College of Physicians in 1983, and takes into account your frame size and sex. If you weigh more than 10% over the standard weight for your height you are overweight; more than 20% and you are very overweight. If you have a large frame, your weight will be near the top of the range, and near the bottom if you have a small frame size. Judge your frame size by the breadth of shoulders and size of hands and feet. Chart B is known as the *Body Mass Index* or *Quetelet Index*, and works by comparing height to weight according to a formula. Use the following scoring system for chart B:

0 = not overweight      2 = very overweight

1 = overweight      3 = extremely overweight

# A – WEIGHT RECOMMENDATIONS

Women

| | Height | | | Weight | | | | |
|---|---|---|---|---|---|---|---|---|
| ft in | m | | st | lb | st | lb | kg | kg |
| 4 10 | 1.45 | | 6 | 8 – | 8 | 7 | 42 – 53 | |
| 4 11 | 1.50 | | 6 | 10 – | 8 | 10 | 43 – 55 | |
| 5 0 | 1.52 | | 6 | 12 – | 8 | 13 | 44 – 57 | |
| 5 1 | 1.56 | | 7 | 1 – | 9 | 1 | 45 – 58 | |
| 5 2 | 1.58 | | 7 | 3 – | 9 | 3 | 46 – 59 | |
| 5 3 | 1.60 | | 7 | 7 – | 9 | 8 | 48 – 61 | |
| 5 4 | 1.62 | | 7 | 9 – | 9 | 10 | 49 – 62 | |
| 5 5 | 1.64 | | 7 | 12 – | 10 | 0 | 50 – 64 | |
| 5 6 | 1.68 | | 8 | 2 – | 10 | 5 | 52 – 66 | |
| 5 7 | 1.70 | | 8 | 4 – | 10 | 7 | 53 – 67 | |
| 5 8 | 1.72 | | 8 | 9 – | 10 | 11 | 55 – 69 | |
| 5 9 | 1.74 | | 8 | 13 – | 11 | 2 | 57 – 71 | |
| 5 10 | 1.78 | | 9 | 3 – | 11 | 8 | 59 – 74 | |

Men

| | Height | | | Weight | | | | |
|---|---|---|---|---|---|---|---|---|
| ft in | m | | st | lb | st | lb | kg | kg |
| 5 3 | 1.60 | | 8 | 2 – | 10 | 3 | 52 – 65 | |
| 5 4 | 1.62 | | 8 | 4 – | 10 | 5 | 53 – 66 | |
| 5 5 | 1.64 | | 8 | 6 – | 10 | 7 | 54 – 67 | |
| 5 6 | 1.68 | | 8 | 11 – | 11 | 2 | 56 – 71 | |
| 5 7 | 1.70 | | 9 | 1 – | 11 | 6 | 58 – 73 | |
| 5 8 | 1.72 | | 9 | 3 – | 11 | 8 | 59 – 74 | |
| 5 9 | 1.74 | | 9 | 8 – | 11 | 13 | 61 – 76 | |
| 5 10 | 1.78 | | 10 | 0 – | 12 | 5 | 64 – 79 | |
| 5 11 | 1.80 | | 10 | 3 – | 12 | 8 | 65 – 80 | |
| 6 0 | 1.84 | | 10 | 7 – | 13 | 2 | 67 – 84 | |
| 6 1 | 1.86 | | 10 | 11 – | 13 | 7 | 69 – 86 | |
| 6 2 | 1.88 | | 11 | 2 – | 13 | 11 | 71 – 88 | |
| 6 3 | 1.90 | | 11 | 9 – | 14 | 6 | 74 – 92 | |

*Reproduced with permission from:* Obesity. *A report of a working party of the Royal College of Physicians, 1983.*

# B – YOUR BODY MASS INDEX

## Weight

| st | lb | kg | 4 10 / 1.45 | 4 11 / 1.50 | 5 / 1.52 | 5 1 / 1.56 | 5 2 / 1.58 | 5 3 / 1.60 | 5 4 / 1.62 | 5 5 / 1.64 | 5 6 / 1.68 | 5 7 / 1.70 | 5 8 / 1.72 | 5 9 / 1.74 | 5 10 / 1.78 | 5 11 / 1.80 | 6 / 1.84 |
|----|----|----|---|---|---|---|---|---|---|---|---|---|---|---|---|---|---|
| 15 | 1  | 96 | 3 | 3 | 3 | 2 | 2 | 2 | 2 | 2 | 2 | 2 | 2 | 2 | 2 | 1 | 1 |
| 14 | 10 | 93 | 3 | 3 | 2 | 2 | 2 | 2 | 2 | 2 | 2 | 2 | 2 | 2 | 1 | 1 | 1 |
| 14 | 8  | 92 | 3 | 3 | 2 | 2 | 2 | 2 | 2 | 2 | 2 | 2 | 2 | 2 | 1 | 1 | 1 |
| 14 | 2  | 90 | 3 | 2 | 2 | 2 | 2 | 2 | 2 | 2 | 2 | 2 | 2 | 2 | 1 | 1 | 1 |
| 13 | 13 | 88 | 3 | 2 | 2 | 2 | 2 | 2 | 2 | 2 | 2 | 2 | 1 | 1 | 1 | 1 | 1 |
| 13 | 7  | 86 | 3 | 2 | 2 | 2 | 2 | 2 | 2 | 2 | 2 | 1 | 1 | 1 | 1 | 1 | 1 |
| 13 | 2  | 83 | 3 | 2 | 2 | 2 | 2 | 2 | 2 | 2 | 2 | 1 | 1 | 1 | 1 | 1 | 1 |
| 12 | 12 | 82 | 2 | 2 | 2 | 2 | 2 | 2 | 2 | 2 | 1 | 1 | 1 | 1 | 1 | 1 | 0 |
| 12 | 8  | 80 | 2 | 2 | 2 | 2 | 2 | 2 | 2 | 1 | 1 | 1 | 1 | 1 | 1 | 0 | 0 |
| 12 | 3  | 77 | 2 | 2 | 2 | 2 | 2 | 2 | 1 | 1 | 1 | 1 | 1 | 1 | 0 | 0 | 0 |
| 11 | 13 | 76 | 2 | 2 | 2 | 2 | 2 | 1 | 1 | 1 | 1 | 1 | 1 | 0 | 0 | 0 | 0 |
| 11 | 8  | 73 | 2 | 2 | 2 | 2 | 1 | 1 | 1 | 1 | 1 | 1 | 0 | 0 | 0 | 0 | 0 |
| 11 | 4  | 72 | 2 | 2 | 2 | 2 | 1 | 1 | 1 | 1 | 1 | 0 | 0 | 0 | 0 | 0 | 0 |
| 11 | 0  | 70 | 2 | 2 | 2 | 1 | 1 | 1 | 1 | 1 | 1 | 0 | 0 | 0 | 0 | 0 | 0 |
| 10 | 9  | 67 | 2 | 1 | 1 | 1 | 1 | 1 | 1 | 0 | 0 | 0 | 0 | 0 | 0 | 0 | 0 |
| 10 | 5  | 66 | 2 | 1 | 1 | 1 | 1 | 1 | 0 | 0 | 0 | 0 | 0 | 0 | 0 | 0 | 0 |
| 10 | 0  | 63 | 2 | 1 | 1 | 1 | 1 | 1 | 0 | 0 | 0 | 0 | 0 | 0 | 0 | 0 | 0 |
| 9  | 10 | 62 | 2 | 1 | 1 | 1 | 1 | 0 | 0 | 0 | 0 | 0 | 0 | 0 | 0 | 0 | 0 |
| 9  | 6  | 60 | 1 | 1 | 1 | 1 | 0 | 0 | 0 | 0 | 0 | 0 | 0 | 0 | 0 | 0 | 0 |
| 9  | 1  | 57 | 1 | 1 | 0 | 0 | 0 | 0 | 0 | 0 | 0 | 0 | 0 | 0 | 0 | 0 | 0 |
| 8  | 13 | 56 | 1 | 0 | 0 | 0 | 0 | 0 | 0 | 0 | 0 | 0 | 0 | 0 | 0 | 0 | 0 |
| 8  | 8  | 54 | 1 | 0 | 0 | 0 | 0 | 0 | 0 | 0 | 0 | 0 | 0 | 0 | 0 | 0 | 0 |
| 8  | 3  | 52 | 0 | 0 | 0 | 0 | 0 | 0 | 0 | 0 | 0 | 0 | 0 | 0 | 0 | 0 | 0 |

ft & in / m

## Height

*Adapted from* Obesity and Related Diseases *by J. S. Garrow, published* Churchill Livingstone, 1983.

# *What kind of diet would suit me best?*

Any diet you go on will need to be much lower in calories than what you normally eat. Most slimming diets contain 1,000 calories less than you need. The reason for this is that 2lbs of body fat contains 7,000 calories. So you will need to eat 1,000 fewer calories each day, in order to lose around 2lbs a week on your diet.

People lose weight at a faster or slower rate, depending on their age, sex, and physical activity. Most lose more weight during their first week on a diet, because of water loss. One to two pounds is a normal healthy amount to lose each week. If you are losing a lot more than this, e.g. 7lbs a week, you will not be losing just fat, but also muscle.

There are *four diet plans*. They have been designed to cover all the different types of jobs women do, from running a home to jetting around the world. Each diet plan suggests which occupations it might be most suitable for. Their calorie limit is based on the amount of activity people in those professions normally use. If you exercise a lot, you might lose weight on a higher calorie diet plan than your occupation dictates. Most women would lose weight on any of these diets. But their calorie content is a little on the low side for men.

Don't allow a slimming diet to dictate how you live your life. YOUR UNIQUE LIFE STYLE DIET LETS YOU LIVE LIFE TO THE FULL WHILST HELPING YOU LOSE WEIGHT AND STAY SLIM. If you are not sure which diet you should choose, or want to discover more about your personal dietary profile, answer this quiz.

# Quiz

The following twenty questions are designed to reveal your dietary identity. Tick the answer closest to your life style.

## A – YOUR WORKING DAY

### 1 *What do you normally have for breakfast?*

A I rarely eat breakfast. I don't feel hungry early and it doesn't fit into my schedule.

B No breakfast – but I grab a scone at the snack bar the moment I get to work.

C I like a healthy start – fruit juice, muesli and coffee with skimmed milk.

D Cereal and something cooked. Everyone needs a proper breakfast.

E Coffee and cereal, but bacon, sausage and all the trimmings are a weekend treat.

### 2 *Do you eat during the morning?*

A Yes – a couple of biscuits to keep me going.

B No – just coffee with milk.

C Yes – I buy a banana for a mid-morning snack.

D Yes – I enjoy a cup of freshly brewed coffee and biscuits.

E Yes – I always have a hot drink and a plain biscuit.

### 3 *What do you do for lunch?*

A Work doesn't stop because it is 1 o'clock. I have a sandwich at my desk but often work through.

B I always have half-an-hour for lunch and eat a meat

and two veg lunch in the canteen sometimes followed by a pudding.

C Lunch usually takes place in a wine bar with colleagues or in a restaurant with business associates.

D I go to the local veggie bar because they have the best salads.

E I have no set lunch routine. I might grab a burger or make do with a packet of cheesey snack biscuits.

## 4 *What happens in the afternoon?*

A Usually somebody brews up tea and passes round the biscuits or cakes.

B I always have tea at 4 p.m.

C I grab a cup of tea in between appointments.

D I'll probably eat a cereal bar with lemon or fruit tea.

E Tea at teatime with crisps or a bar of chocolate.

## 5 *On my way home . . .*

A I eat a wholewheat muffin and fruit juice at the station.

B I nibble on nuts in the pub after work.

C I don't leave work until late. I usually buy a snack on the way home.

D I always have my meal at 6 p.m., so I eat nothing.

E I pick at olives and other freebies in the wine bar.

## 6 *When I get home . . .*

A I stick a ready meal in the microwave.

B I have some cheese on toast. I often have a takeaway later on.

C I start to cook the evening meal – usually meat and two veg.

D I eat fresh fruit or nibble on the vegetables I am preparing for my meal.

E I have a gin and tonic and decide what to have for dinner.

7 **If I could eat anything when I went out for a meal I'd choose:**
A Champagne and smoked salmon.
B Vegetarian thali at a really good Indian.
C Roast beef at one of those carveries.
D Lots of different things at one of those amazing open air buffets now put on by so many hotels abroad.
E A really good fish or seafood dish in a top notch French restaurant – in France!

# B – YOUR PHILOSOPHY ON DIET AND EXERCISE

1 **Food is:**
A Necessary but shouldn't interfere with the working day.
B Something I am always eating.
C Best eaten at regular intervals three times a day.
D Good for you or very bad for you depending on how you pick.
E An enjoyable part of my social life. Good food is important.

2 **If I have an eating problem, it is:**
A There doesn't seem to be time to fit in every meal.
B People tell me I eat far more than they do.
C It is hard to find a canteen meal or café that does not serve overprocessed rubbish.
D Everything I like other people say is fattening.
E I really hate to eat on my own.

**3 *My view of convenience food is:***

A Something to be avoided – it is unhealthy.

B Useful because I never have time to cook, but eat it sometimes.

C Not something I would give to the family.

D I would have to be desperate to eat it.

E It is something I eat a lot of.

**4 *My favourite snack is:***

A A piece of cheese or cheese and biscuits.

B Sweet biscuits or cake.

C Crisps and nuts.

D A bar of chocolate.

E Fresh fruit or a low fat yoghurt.

**5 *The healthiest meal on this list is:***

A Cheese salad.

B Smoked salmon sandwich.

C Vegetable lasagne.

D Roast chicken dinner.

E Low calorie chilled meal.

**6 *My view of exercise is:***

A I get all I need hurrying to work and being busy.

B I work out at the gym twice a week.

C Try running around after three children – that's all the exercise you need.

D I try to play squash once a week.

E My parents never took any and they weren't over-weight.

**7 *If I did exercise it would be:***

A Squash.

B Dancing.

C  A brisk walk.
D  A jog around the park.
E  Aerobics.

# C – YOUR VIEW OF YOUR WEIGHT AND DIETING

### 1 *I want to lose weight because:*
A  Fat people get missed for promotion.
B  A little weight is OK but too much is ageing.
C  It is unhealthy to be overweight.
D  Nobody loves a fat girl.
E  I want to get into a size 10.

### 2 *Which statement do you most agree with:*
A  My weight is entirely my own responsibility.
B  Most of the food I normally eat is not allowed on a diet.
C  When I make up my mind to diet I do it.
D  If everyone is on a diet too it is a great help.
E  Deciding which diet to go on is the most difficult part.

### 3 *Looking at my body in the mirror:*
A  I think I need to lose half a stone.
B  I look pretty good, but see room for improvement.
C  I see a shameful spare tyre.
D  Is that really me?
E  I decide to skip the next two business lunches.

### 4 *When I start a diet I feel:*
A  Eager to get on with it.
B  Fed up, but realise it is necessary.
C  This time it will work.

D Certain I will be doing the same thing this time next
year.
E Determined I can change my eating patterns.

**5 *I bought this book because:***
A I try out every new diet.
B There is a diet to suit my life style.
C I can give it to my friend.
D This time I will succeed.
E I have not got time to work out a diet for myself.

**6 *The clothes I most long to wear are:***
A Levi 501s and an Armani T-shirt.
B A genuine Chanel suit and matching shoes.
C A Bruce Oldfield ball gown.
D A Jaeger suit.
E Leggings and a leotard from Pineapple.

# HOW TO SCORE

| Section | A | | | | | B | | | | | C | | | | |
|---|---|---|---|---|---|---|---|---|---|---|---|---|---|---|---|
| *Question* | A | B | C | D | E | A | B | C | D | E | A | B | C | D | E |
| 1 | 7 | 3 | 9 | 5 | 1 | 5 | 3 | 1 | 7 | 9 | 1 | 7 | 9 | 5 | 3 |
| 2 | 3 | 1 | 9 | 7 | 5 | 1 | 5 | 9 | 3 | 7 | 9 | 3 | 1 | 7 | 5 |
| 3 | 1 | 5 | 7 | 9 | 3 | 9 | 1 | 5 | 7 | 3 | 9 | 1 | 5 | 3 | 7 |
| 4 | 7 | 5 | 1 | 9 | 3 | 7 | 5 | 3 | 1 | 9 | 1 | 7 | 5 | 3 | 9 |
| 5 | 9 | 3 | 1 | 5 | 7 | 1 | 7 | 9 | 5 | 3 | 5 | 7 | 3 | 9 | 1 |
| 6 | 1 | 3 | 5 | 9 | 7 | 1 | 9 | 5 | 7 | 3 | 3 | 1 | 7 | 5 | 9 |
| 7 | 3 | 7 | 5 | 1 | 9 | 7 | 3 | 5 | 1 | 9 | | | | | |

If you scored:

**Less than 30** – eating is not especially important to you. Your time is mainly taken up with work. If lunchtime cuts across a meeting you will not eat then. So why are you overweight? Well you probably stuff a lot of snack foods without really noticing that as well as convenient they are also high in calories. Also if you eat nothing all day and have a large, late evening meal, you are in danger of lowering your BMR. You need to woo yourself onto a more sensible regime. You are too busy to take much exercise, but never have much time to sit down at work. Because you rely a lot on convenience and snack foods, the *Odd Hours diet plan* would suit you best.

**30 to 80** – you are a lazy eater. You do not bother with meals, but fill up on snacks, especially at work. You often go to the pub for lunch and generally eat what everyone else has, regardless of calorie values. You are not very keen on cooking and often use convenience foods to cook with. You are not very active or sporty, and prefer to go out and have a good social life. You would probably find the *Deskbound diet plan* would suit you best.

**80 to 120** – you have a very set dietary routine. You sensibly like to plan to have three meals daily, and usually prefer traditional fare. You might have a family to cook for. In any case, you like to cook a proper evening meal, and rarely use convenience food. You don't really get much exercise, except taking the dog for a walk. The *At Home diet plan* is probably the one you should go for.

***120 to 160*** – you appreciate good food and see it as one of the pleasures in life. You go out for dinner a lot, enjoy lunch and evening sessions in the wine bar, and are often away at weekends. Your job is not very active, but you try to get some regular exercise. You often fit a game of tennis or squash into your social life, and enjoy country walks at weekends. The *Traveller's diet plan* is the one for you.

***160 to 180*** – you are very aware of your food, and try very hard to eat a healthy diet. You are very knowledgeable about fibre and your diet will never be short of the necessary vitamins and minerals. You avoid all convenience food and takeaways, because you feel they are not good for you. You try to get as much exercise as possible, and do some sort of serious workout once a week. You do not really have a serious weight problem and so may find the *Traveller's diet plan* the best for you. Just remember that foods that are 'good for you' can be just as high in calories as any other.

# What you should do before starting your diet

Successful diets are ones planned well in advance. Deciding to go on a diet is a good first step; you are taking responsibility for your own problems. But once you have made that decision get on with it! Don't put it off until next week, because you have got a conference in Italy this week, or your wedding anniversary is tomorrow. *Your Life Style Diet* gives you tips on how to cope with difficult situations.

Tell family, friends and work colleagues about your diet and get them on your side. These days people rarely try to tempt you off your diet by sticking boxes of chocolates under your nose. Make sure they understand what you are trying to do and why. Be positive about this diet. Show people you can still enjoy life because on this diet you don't have to become a social outcast. They might even want to try your diet themselves. But if you don't want anyone to know you are on a diet, don't tell them – they'll never guess. The beauty of *Your Life Style Diet* is that you can eat normal food. No one need ever know you are dieting, until your new, slimmer shape gives the game away.

Plan how you are going to monitor your success. Ideally you should weigh yourself once a week or fortnight. Set yourself a realistic goal for your final target weight or you will be disappointed. Be wary of instant changes in your weight, they are most likely to be caused by water loss or gain.

You might reach a point where your weight plateaus and stays the same for two or three weeks. If this is happening to you don't abandon the diet in despair. You will start to lose weight again eventually. Don't get complacent about your diet and start cutting corners, or adding in a few extra bits and pieces. If you are stuck at a certain weight, read your diet plan again and compare what you should be eating to what you are actually eating.

Set some other goals besides your target weight. Wearing a bikini on holiday, buying some new clothes without feeling humiliated in the communal changing room, getting into and looking good in some Levi 501s, treating yourself to a good holiday after you have kept to your target weight for more than six months, taking up squash or tennis or touching your toes. Make up your own list of things dear to your heart that losing weight could help you achieve.

Organise your weekly shop and make sure you do not have tempting foods lying around. You will also need to decide what to do in an emergency situation, when you cannot avoid eating foods not on your diet plan. Don't let guilty feelings give you an excuse to stop dieting. Eating high calorie foods occasionally will not increase your overall calorie intake enough to ruin your diet.

Before you start this diet, remember how much dieting affects your metabolism and make this diet your last. Keep to your diet plan until you have lost the weight you want, then plan life after your diet (see pages 95–104). Keeping your weight at a reasonable level means you have to make some lasting changes to your food intake. Avoid being constantly on and off diets. Otherwise you could permanently lower your metabolism and be chained to your calorie counter for life.

Think carefully about why you want to lose weight, and what being slimmer will mean for you personally. There can be many reasons why people eat too much. Will losing the fat you have accumulated by overeating solve all your problems?

Finally, do not believe everything people tell you about food and diets. There are many old wives' tales about which foods are good/bad for you and which foods you can and cannot have on a diet. The problem is that there are many conflicting and confusing messages about food and health around. The next few pages will try and provide answers to questions you might have.

# BEFORE YOU START YOUR DIET – CHECKLIST

1 Plan how you are going to go about your diet.
2 Don't put your diet off until next week. Start to-morrow.
3 Tell family, friends and work colleagues about your diet.
4 Decide what weight you want to be – use the charts.
5 Plan how you are going to monitor your diet.
6 Set some other goals besides your target weight.
7 Organise your food shopping.
8 Be aware about guilt from eating high calorie foods – plan how you are going to deal with it.
9 Think about what being slimmer will mean for you.
10 Disregard old wives' tales and well-meaning advice from friends.
11 Make a resolution that this must be your last diet.

# *Healthy Eating*

Means having less fat, sugar and salt in your diet and more fibre-rich starchy foods.

Today there is a bewildering variety of foods to choose from. Sometimes it is hard to know what to eat for the best. A lot of it has been processed leaving us little preparation or cooking to do. Because of this it is easy to eat more processed food than is good for us. On the other hand, it can save us from those high calorie foods nibbled to stave off hunger pangs whilst waiting for our evening meal to cook. So don't feel bad about eating

processed food. It can be just as nutritious as fresh food
. . . and as full of calories and hidden fat!

Whether it is processed or fresh, the food we eat
should provide us with a balanced intake of protein, fat,
carbohydrates, vitamins and minerals to stay healthy.
One hundred years ago we ate half as much fat and
twice as much carbohydrate as we do today. Experts
think that this could be one reason why diseases such as
heart disease are more common today.

EAT FEWER fried foods, crisps, nuts, oils, fats, salad
dressings, biscuits and chocolates and less pastry, full
cream milk, Cheddar-type cheese, cream cheese, red
meat, sausages and luncheon meat.

FILL UP ON starchy high fibre foods such as bread,
potatoes, pasta, rice, cereals, fruit and vegetables.

SUGAR is high in calories, and causes tooth decay.
Don't eat many sweets, chocolates, cakes, biscuits,
puddings and don't drink fizzy drinks.

SALT is OK in moderation. Add a little to your cooking
but keep the salt cellar off the table.

# Good and Bad Foods

*Don't think of food in terms of being good or bad for you*. This
has the effect of making you feel very guilty when you
eat a 'bad' food. Try to think of food as being either a
high fat/sugar food or a low fat/sugar food. Your diet
should consist of mostly low fat/sugar foods, but eating
a small number of high fat/sugar foods will not be fatal.
*Your Life Style Diet* includes such foods on a weekly
treats list, so eat and enjoy them.

*Foods classed as 'good', 'healthy' or 'natural', can be quite high in fat or sugar.* The types of foods which have this 'healthy' label, include yoghurt, honey, muesli and other breakfast cereals high in nuts and dried fruit, fruit juice, and high fibre foods such as wholemeal biscuits. Check the labels carefully before you buy foods. Most will give you the number of calories per serving as well as fat and sugar – see the list of healthy and unhealthy foods.

*Convenience food is often thought of as junk food, but this is not always the case.* It can be just as good for you as homemade food, and sometimes it contains less fat and calories. Working women find convenience food very useful, so don't feel guilty about eating it. It makes life easier for us all. If you eat a lot of convenience and takeaway food, try to have a freshly cooked meal once or twice a week, and a helping of fruit and vegetables daily. Knowing which convenience foods you can eat on a diet is not a problem. *Your Life Style Diet* includes them in your diet plan and in the calorie counter.

# HEALTHY AND UNHEALTHY FOODS

## Healthy?

## Unhealthy?

| Healthy? | Unhealthy? |
|---|---|
| *Fruit yoghurt – low fat* (125g) 112 calories 22 grams sugar | *Tub dairy icecream* (60g) 116 calories 12 grams sugar |
| *Unsweetened natural orange juice* (Glass 200mls) 65 calories 17 grams sugar | *Lemonade* (Glass 200mls) 41 calories 12 grams sugar |

Bowl cornflakes
146 calories
Portion sunflower margarine
51 calories
Small bag mixed nuts and raisins
(1oz or 30g)
134 calories
13 grams fat
10 grams sugar
*Cereal bar* (average of 3 brands)
116 calories
*Wholemeal bran biscuits* (2)
120 calories
Flapjack
120 calories
Teaspoon honey
57 calories
15 grams sugar

Bowl sugar-free muesli
256 calories
Portion butter
51 calories
Fruit pastilles

(Half a packet – 20g)
50 calories
0 grams fat
12 grams sugar
*Jaffa cakes* (2)

86 calories
*Cream crackers* (2)
61 calories
Chocolate mini roll
87 calories
Teaspoon jam
52 calories
14 grams sugar

# Diet Facts and Fiction

None of these old wives' tales about diets and slimming is true.

*Grapefruit burns up fat.*
Grapefruit are very low in calories but do not have any magical slimming properties. Use them to bulk out your diet. Also eating any sour fruit will make other foods taste extra sweet, and help get rid of a love of sweet things.

*Salads are slimming.*

Like cooked vegetables, salad vegetables are very low in calories. Eating large quantities on a diet will help to fill you up. Salads only stay low in calories if they do not have any high calorie dressings on, or contain nuts, olives and dried fruit.

*Eating nothing all day helps you lose weight.*

Many people believe they eat nothing all day. They either conveniently forget about those nibbles, or they starve themselves so they can eat a large meal at night. Snacks can be very high in calories – see page 41, and starvation lowers your BMR. You might find you eat more food on a diet than you would do normally, and still lose weight. It is not how much you eat that counts, but what you eat and when.

*Margarine is lower in calories than butter.*

Margarine contains the same number of calories as butter, unless it is a low fat spread. The same applies to cooking oils and lard. Fried food will still be high in calories and fat whatever you use.

*Honey is better for you than sugar.*

Honey is sugar by another name. It is just as high in calories as jam or marmalade, so treat it in the same way.

*Cutting out meat is a good idea if you are on a diet.*

There is no need to stop eating red meat, whatever diet you are on. Just be careful to buy lean meat and only eat small amounts. Eat more chicken and fish, rather than having red meat daily.

*You should have lots of fresh fruit and fruit juice on a diet.*

Fruit is not calorie free and some types can be quite high in calories e.g. bananas and grapes. It is useful as a between-meal filler, but stick to your allowance. Fruit juice, even the unsweetened kind, is quite high in calories. Avoid it unless it is part of your diet.

*To lose weight you must cut out bread and potatoes.*

As a nation we eat too much meat and not enough starchy foods such as bread and potatoes, so never stop eating them on your diet. Compared to rice or pasta they contain fewer calories and more valuable nutrients such as iron, protein and Vitamin C.

*Low calorie salad cream, biscuits, icecream and jam are OK to eat on a diet.*

Low calorie does not mean no calorie. Some diet foods are not much lower in calories than ordinary foods. Read the labels and compare the calorie values of diet and ordinary foods. If you want to eat biscuits and icecream, have something from your treats list.

*Diabetic foods are fine for slimmers.*

Diabetic foods may not contain sugar, but usually have other ingredients which make them too high in calories for slimmers.

# WHAT'S IN A NIBBLE?

| | |
|---|---|
| Mini pork pie (50g) | 188 calories |
| Mini sausage roll (21g) | 100 calories |
| 2 crackers + butter pat | 113 calories |
| Small bag/handful nuts | 142 calories |
| 2 digestive biscuits | 141 calories |
| Piece of fruit cake | 247 calories |
| Cube cheese (1oz) | 121 calories |
| Mince pie | 243 calories |
| 4 dates | 148 calories |
| 2 oatcakes + 1oz cheese | 235 calories |
| Scone + butter & jam | 250 calories |

# 2 *Introducing Your Diet Plan*

## *Points to Watch*

## MILK

All diets include an allowance of ⅓ pint of ordinary or semi-skimmed milk, which is probably enough for six cups of tea or coffee a day. If you want more than six cups of tea or coffee with milk in you will have to use skimmed milk only. Milk on cereals, three tablespoons, is included in the calorie count for breakfast, and is therefore separate.

## TREATS LIST

Every life style diet has an allowance of 350 calories a week to use for high fat, high sugar foods. This is to help make the diet more flexible and fun. Generally you will be allowed four items from your treats list every week.

## BREAKFAST

Try if possible to eat high fibre wholegrain breakfast cereals and wholemeal bread. Also be sparing with the milk you add to cereals. For the higher calorie plans, ordinary milk is acceptable, but if you are on 1,000 calories a day, you should be using semi-skimmed or skimmed milk on cereal. Low fat spread is the best spread to use on toast or bread, but still spread it very thinly.

## SNACK MEAL

When buying sandwiches, try to get wholemeal or granary ones if possible. Also be careful that they do not contain a lot of butter or any mayonnaise/salad cream. If you are making your own sandwiches always use a low fat spread and granary/wholemeal bread.

## MAIN MEAL

Avoid fried foods, any with cream in or on, and pastry in all forms. Although oven chips have been included in all the options, they are still higher in calories and fat than boiled or jacket potatoes. Only have them once or twice a week at the most. All options have been calorie counted to include a large portion of vegetables.

Chilled and frozen ready meals are included in all the diet plans. Most if not all have the calorie value per serving marked on the pack. Provided you stick to that portion size, you know how many calories you have eaten. Some people might find these portion sizes a little on the small side.

# LOW CALORIE FOODS

The following foods are low in calories and you do not have to worry about the amount you eat. Use them as fillers, but remember that they have no special slimming powers.

## *Vegetables*

All may be eaten freely, except avocado pears, baked, broad, kidney, and butter beans. Each life style diet allows 50 calories a day for vegetables, so make the most of this and have plenty.

## *Fruit*

Grapefruit, gooseberries, blackberries, blackcurrants, raspberries and rhubarb can be eaten in large amounts. Sweeten only if necessary, using an artificial sweetener.

## *Miscellaneous*

Clear soups, meat and yeast extracts, tea, coffee, tomato

juice, spring water, soda water, low calorie fizzy drinks, and low calorie fruit squash, can be included in your diet.

## Artificial Sweeteners

These are fine to have on a diet, but make sure they are not the sort that contain some sugar. There are many different types, so buy one to suit your taste and your purse. However, *it is better to give up sugar in tea and coffee altogether*, and get used to everything tasting less sweet.

# 3 *The Traveller's Diet*

This diet contains 1,200 calories, and is designed for women who travel and eat meals away from home a good deal. It would be suitable for saleswomen, business women, air stewardesses, lawyers, couriers, singers, dancers, actresses and long distance commuters. It has a higher calorie value than the other diets, to suit women on the move and accommodate those business lunches.

Included in the meal options are foods you can choose whilst staying in a hotel, travelling on a train or plane, or eating out in a restaurant. This diet plan takes into account the fact that you might often have little choice about where you eat. It also appreciates that entertaining or being entertained is often part of your job, and not something you can stop doing just because you are on a diet.

The treats list will also help you cope with this aspect of your work – when you cannot refuse a glass of champagne offered by a client, or need to eat a biscuit during a meeting to keep you going because you do not know how long it will be until your next meal. Your treats are also for comfort eating, when you need to relax over a gin and tonic, or flop on the couch with jet lag and only some chocolate will do.

If your job involves travel but is otherwise very sedentary, then choose one of the lower calorie diet plans.

# Diet Plan                    **1,200 calories**

## BREAKFAST                    **200 calories**

Choose one of the following:
- 1 rasher bacon + poached egg + grilled tomatoes and ½ slice bread (dry)
- 2 slices toast + scrape butter
- 2" piece French bread + 1oz Camembert/Brie cheese
- 3" piece French bread + butter pat or jam portion
- 1 croissant
- 1 chipolata sausage + 1 rasher bacon + grilled tomatoes
- Variety pack cornflakes/branflakes + milk + 1 piece toast + scrape butter
- Choose one item from list A and one from list B

*List A*
2 Weetabix + milk
Small bowl All-Bran +
  milk
Medium bowl
  cornflakes/branflakes
  + milk
1 slice toast + butter/
  margarine
1 slice toast (dry) +
  boiled egg
1 slice toast (dry) + 2oz
  cottage cheese

*List B*
Fresh fruit
Bowl stewed prunes
Bowl fruit salad
Low fat plain yoghurt
Diet fruit yoghurt
Low fat fromage frais

## SNACK MEAL                    **350 calories**

Choose one of the following:
- Beefburger or cheeseburger + carton of fruit juice
  e.g. hamburger or cheeseburger from Burger King,
  McDonald's or Wimpy
- Portion shepherd's pie and vegetables
- Portion chilli con carne and vegetables (no rice)
- Ham, prawn, beef or chicken salad with a small roll
  or 3" piece French bread (no butter) + bowl soup or
  piece fruit
- Small slice quiche or mini pizza or small peppered
  mackerel and salad + bowl soup or diet yoghurt.
- Salad bowl – 1 portion bean salad, 1 portion mixed
  salad, 1 portion rice or pasta salad + jacket potato or
  roll. Accompanied either by soup or a glass of fruit
  juice
- Turkey, ham, prawn, egg, crab, salmon, smoked

salmon or cottage cheese & salad sandwich with a piece of fruit

- Bacon, tuna, beef, chicken or tandoori chicken sandwich
- Any shop bought sandwich containing 350 calories or less – see pages 152–154 in the calorie counter
- Plain omelette with salad or vegetables and a glass of fruit juice or a small boiled potato
- 3 crispbread or 3 cream crackers + one of the following:
  1oz Cheddar cheese
  4oz cottage cheese
  individual (40g) portion Camembert
  3 triangles cheese spread
  + a mug or carton of soup and a piece of fresh fruit
- 1 small pitta bread and 2 tablespoons houmous
- Smoked haddock fillet with 1 slice bread & butter + low fat fromage frais or diet yoghurt
- Bacon roll – as purchased
- Jacket potato + small portion butter and baked beans or coleslaw
  e.g. Spud-U-Like – chilli con carne, hot beans, sweetcorn, cottage cheese, tuna salad, prawn cocktail, coleslaw
- 2″ French stick + jumbo sausage
- Greek salad + pitta bread/Greek bread
- Medium-sized vegetable or small meat samosa
- Airline meals – you may eat the main part of the meal e.g. the meat/chicken/fish with vegetables and potatoes/rice/pasta
  + either the bread roll + butter *or* crackers and cheese portion + dessert *or* starter

# MAIN MEAL                                    **500 calories**

## *Eating at home*

### Home cooking
*Either* – choose one item from list A, and one from list B. With this you may have unlimited salad or cooked vegetables. You may have, in addition, either a bowl of vegetable soup to start, or a dessert of fresh fruit, a portion of sugar-free tinned fruit, a diet fruit yoghurt or low fat fromage frais.

### *List A*
Roast chicken leg/breast
3oz roast beef/lamb/pork
6oz grilled cod/plaice
Small pork/lamb chop
2 grilled beefburgers
2 rashers grilled back
  bacon
2 eggs not fried
4oz liver (raw weight)
Grilled steak (6oz raw)
Grilled trout
4oz poached salmon
4 grilled fish fingers
2 grilled chipolata
  sausages
6 tablespoons cooked
  lentils
2oz Cheddar cheese

### *List B*
4 small boiled potatoes
  (8oz)
1 large jacket potato
  (8oz)
4oz oven chips
2oz pasta (raw weight)
4 tablespoons boiled rice
½ packet savoury rice
2 slices bread + scrape
4 tablespoons baked
  beans
4 tablespoons tinned
  spaghetti
6 tablespoons cooked
  beans

*Or* – any of the special recipe dishes given on pages 106 to 128. Accompanying the meal you may have a bowl of soup to start and fresh fruit, or sugar-free tinned fruit, or diet yoghurt or low fat fromage frais for dessert.

## Chilled or frozen ready meals

You may have any chilled or frozen meal under 500 calories. Choose from the ones given in your calorie counter on pages 135–141. If you have one containing less than 400 calories you may have, in addition, a large helping of vegetables and some fresh or tinned sugar-free fruit *or* a slice of bread and low fat spread.


## *Eating out*

This section is divided up into different types of meals you would get in a hotel/restaurant/takeaway. It is difficult to generalise about restaurant food as portion sizes can vary a great deal. If the amount on your plate looks a lot, then leave some.

## Hotel or French restaurant

You may choose *either* to have a starter and main meal *or* dessert and main meal from the ones listed below. If you want a glass of wine with your meal, have one from your treats allowance. Do not eat the bread or bread sticks on the table, unless you intend having only a main course.

## Starters

Bowl vegetable soup
Melon – either on its
   own or with Parma
   ham
Fruit cocktail
Vegetable terrine
Moules marinières
Seafood platter/
   langoustines (avoid
   mayonnaise dips)
Smoked salmon
½ grapefruit

## Desserts

Fresh fruit salad
Sorbet
Fresh fruit
Crème caramel
Mousse

## Main courses

You can eat any of the following with a serving of vegetables or salad – ask for your vegetables without butter and salad without dressing. Do not have any rice or potatoes with your meal, unless you are only having a main meal and no starter/dessert.

Poached/grilled fish or seafood – avoid cream/alcohol sauces if possible, but if you have no option try to leave most of it. A tomato sauce is fine.
Game – venison/partridge/pheasant/rabbit – eat a minimum of any sauce served with any of these.
Steak – choose the smallest one on offer.
Casseroles/stews: chicken/turkey – avoid fried chicken/chicken Kiev etc.
Avoid – duck, anything cooked with cream/alcohol, anything in a pastry case, anything with pâté in it.

# Indian restaurant – either sit down or takeaway

No starter or dessert but you may have one poppadum if you like them.

## Main course

Chicken or lamb tikka or small tandoori chicken
+ salad and half a portion plain boiled rice

# Chinese restaurant – sit down or takeaway

## Starter

Chicken or vegetable soup

## Main course

Chicken or beef chow mein or chop suey with Chinese vegetables

Beef or chicken dish e.g. chicken and mushrooms or beef in black bean sauce with 2 tablespoons boiled rice

Avoid – sweet and sour dishes, dishes with nuts in, any pork dish including spare ribs, prawn crackers.

# English restaurant

You may have one of the following starters or desserts with a main course.

## Starters/Desserts

Fruit cocktail
Fruit salad
Melon
Sorbet

## Main course

Small steak + salad + ½ jacket potato
Gammon steak + salad + ½ jacket potato
Chicken breast + salad + ½ jacket potato

Plaice in breadcrumbs + a jacket potato
If you have not had a starter then you can have a whole jacket potato with some butter. If you are having chicken you may find that the portion size is half a chicken. If this is the case, just eat the breast.

## Takeaways

- Large doner kebab
- Any beefburger up to and including quarterpounder e.g. Burger King hamburger, cheeseburger, double cheeseburger, deluxe cheeseburger. McDonald's hamburger, cheeseburger, quarterpounder, quarterpounder with cheese, Big Mac. Wimpy hamburger, cheeseburger, kingsize
- Jacket potato + any filling e.g. any Spud-U-Like except egg and cheese
- Half of most traditional or deep pan pizzas Whole 5″ deep pan or 7″ traditional Pizzaland pizza Whole thin 'n' crispy Country Feast, Seafarer or Hawaiian Pizza Hut pizza

# TREATS LIST                    **350 calories a week**

You may have two items from list A and two from list B.

*List A*
1 glass wine
2 glasses low alcohol wine
½ pint beer/lager
1 pint low alcohol lager
1 pub measure spirits

*List B*
1 chocolate digestive biscuit
2 boxed chocolates
3 squares milk chocolate
1 choc ice
1 scoop icecream

1 small glass sherry
1 glass milk
1 large glass fruit juice
1 fun sized Milky Way
1 treat sized Crunchie/
    Wispa
1 treat sized Double
    Decker
1 treat sized Cadbury's
    Fudge
3 toffees
2 plain biscuits

2 Jaffa cakes
1 individual jam tart
1 fun sized Mars bar/
    Snickers
½oz peanuts (½ small
    bag)
½ small bag crisps
2 pieces fresh fruit
1 banana
1 slice bread
⅔oz Cheddar cheese

# Case Histories

## Six common problems and their solutions

*Q. Ena's company has offices in several large European cities. Sometimes she feels as though she lives on a plane. 'I am either travelling at lunchtime or the airline offers food in any case. What should I do about this when I need to lose weight?'*
*A. You can eat the airline meal as your lunch provided you follow the guidelines given in the snack meal section. But you don't have to eat what the airline provides. If you have already had a meal or you are planning to eat dinner on your arrival, either don't take anything at all, or eat some fruit and a beverage. Turn down all complimentary snacks, fruit juices and alcoholic drinks, and pick only water or low calorie tonic.*

*Q. Doreen travels Intercity once a week. She worries that the meals seem very large and male orientated. 'It would be all right if my allowance was 2,000 calories a day, but on a diet I am stumped.'*

A. Buffet cars on trains usually have a range of sandwiches. Check on your diet list which are the lowest in calories. Some hot meals could also be suitable. If they have run out of sandwiches, avoid crisps and biscuits and buy a fruit bun or scone and some fresh fruit if you can get it.

Most large railway stations have a reasonable selection of foods. Carry a list with you of what you CAN eat. As a general rule avoid crisps, biscuits, and anything fried or with a lot of butter on it.

If you are going by car for a change, plan to stop at motorway service stations frequently, both for a rest and a snack or meal. It is much better for you and your diet to have regular meals and regular rests.


Q. Jean is a courier who goes abroad frequently and must stay in hotels. She finds such business trips fraught with pitfalls. *'I am supposed to keep an eye on the standard of food provided. I cannot seem to be rejecting everything out of hand.'*

A. Heaven forbid. But there is one thing you can reject . . . your mini-bar fridge in your room . . . unless it contains mineral water. That will be no hardship because many of those drinks seem very highly priced. Keeping alcohol to a minimum is generally a good idea when you are travelling, even if you are not on a diet.

Most hotels serve a continental breakfast which is fine but use your diet list to check whether you are allowed those high fat croissants. If in doubt avoid them. If there is a full breakfast on offer, choose fresh grapefruit or segments in natural juice. Follow this with a boiled egg or poached egg or 2 rashers of grilled bacon + grilled tomato. With this you can *have one slice of toast and a scrape of butter.*

*For the evening meal the simplest thing is to avoid the starter and dessert and you will probably be within your calorie range. Avoid nibbling any bread placed on your table, although one piece is acceptable if you are very hungry. Many hotels now have buffet-style meals which are ideal for the slimmer. If this is the case, go for lots of undressed salads plus grilled meat or fish. Kebabs or barbecued meat and fish are tasty and not too high in calories.*

*Yoghurt is a trap. It is not always low in fat . . . read the label carefully. Greek yoghurt is particularly high in fat. Fresh fruit is often freely available, but beware tropical fruits which can be much higher in calories than apples or pears. Avoid all fruit juices. Generally you can eat as many vegetables as you like. But if your main dish contains pasta or pastry, do not add potatoes, peas or corn.*

*Q. Suzanne says: 'There is always a lot of alcohol on offer in my job. It is very difficult to avoid, especially if I am entertaining clients. When can I drink on this diet? It would look very rude for me to let the client do all the drinking.'*

*A. Really? Designer water is still quite smart and calorie free. You could have a spritzer of dry white wine and soda and make it last. Your treats list allows you a certain number of drinks each week. Try to fit them into your business arrangements. If you are drinking in rounds, miss yourself out when it is your turn. Or buy a fizzy water with ice and lemon, or a tomato juice with ice and lemon. You can always say it is a Bloody Mary. Next round you can ask for a Virgin Mary.*

*Q. Samantha and her girlfriend Julia are going on holiday together to Greece. Neither wants to put on any weight – nor do they want to look like spoil sports.*

A. When you are on holiday, try to strike a happy medium between keeping to your diet and enjoying yourself. The chances are you will be taking far more exercise than usual. This will help counterbalance some of the extra calories you may be eating. The hot weather may help to kill your appetite, but still be careful of the following.

Icecream – having two during your holiday is acceptable, having one every day is not!

Any bar nibbles such as nuts and olives . . . do not let them pass your lips.

Dips and appetisers which start a meal e.g. tzatziki, houmous and aubergine dip are often oily and high in calories.

Olive oil – the natives may add lots to their salads, you should stick to vinegar or lemon juice unless you too are working in the fields!

Honey – may taste more delicious than the honey back home, but it is just as high in calories. Whether you have it with yoghurt or a ground almond pudding it is lethal to any serious diet.

Q. Miranda has to fit in at least two business lunches a week for her city job. She must entertain her clients royally. What on earth can she eat?

A. Make the choice of restaurant one which serves grilled foods and salads. Either go for one main course, starting with a tomato juice and finishing with coffee. Or pick two starters instead of a main meal. Suitable ones could include a citrus fruit cocktail, smoked/pickled fish with salad, melon with Parma ham, fresh vegetable soup, vegetable crudités and yoghurt dip. Avoid cocktail sauces, avocado pears and pâté.

# 4 *The Odd Hours Diet*

This diet contains 1,100 calories each day. It has been designed for women who work irregular hours and cannot be certain of the timing of their meals. It is suitable for nurses, doctors, paramedics, teachers, theatre and cinema workers, bar staff, waitresses and journalists. Many of these jobs involve being on your feet all day. Because of this the calorie allowance is slightly higher.

It is tough having to work when other people are at home with their feet up. To make matters worse, when you do have time for a sit-down meal there is nowhere appealing open. Or all the shops are closed and you cannot buy anything to cook. Your work is also fraught with temptation. People offer you sweets, chocolates or alcoholic drinks. Or perhaps you work with food. What many of you have in common is your lack of control over what you eat and when you eat it. You might have to eat on the run and need something portable. There is often no time for a sit-down meal so you keep yourself going with calorific snacks.

This diet takes into account the limited amount of food available in unsocial hours. We have therefore included a lot of takeaway and chilled convenience food. There are two diet plans you can choose from.

59

One is a traditional breakfast, lunch and dinner. The other is a grazer's plan, giving you the option to have three medium and one small snack meals daily. The foods you can eat are a mixture of fresh and convenience. You have the option to cook at home or eat from the takeaway or freezer.

## *Plan 1*          1,100 calories

## BREAKFAST          150 calories

Choose one of the following:
- 2 Weetabix with skimmed milk
- Medium bowl (50g) All-Bran & skimmed milk
- Small bowl cornflakes & skimmed milk
- Medium bowl (40g) branflakes with skimmed milk
- Small bowl porridge made with 1oz (25g) oats (⅓ mug) & 1 mug skimmed milk
- Low fat plain yoghurt + piece fresh fruit & tablespoon muesli
- 1 slice bread or toast from a medium thick large loaf with a scrape low fat spread and any one of the following:
  Piece fresh fruit (not banana)
  Small bowl stewed dried fruit e.g. prunes
  Mini low fat fromage frais
  Glass unsweetened orange/apple/grapefruit juice
  Small diet fruit yoghurt (125g)
  Scrape Marmite or low sugar jam/marmalade
  Small boiled/poached egg
  2 tablespoons baked beans

# SNACK MEAL                                    **350 calories**

Choose one from:

- Beefburger/cheeseburger (not quarterpounder or larger)
  e.g. hamburger or cheeseburger from Burger King, McDonald's or Wimpy + a piece of fresh fruit (not banana) or glass fresh fruit juice
- Portion shepherd's pie and vegetables or salad + fresh fruit or diet yoghurt or portion vegetable soup
- Portion chilli con carne with vegetables (no rice)
- Ham, prawn, beef or chicken salad with a small roll or 3" piece French bread (no butter) + bowl soup or piece fresh fruit
- Small slice quiche or mini pizza or small peppered mackerel and salad + bowl soup or diet yoghurt
- Salad bowl – 1 portion bean salad, 1 portion mixed salad, 1 portion rice or pasta salad + jacket potato or roll. Accompanied by either bowl soup, glass fruit juice or piece fresh fruit
- Turkey, ham, prawn, crab, salmon, smoked salmon or cottage cheese & salad sandwich with a piece fresh fruit or glass juice
- Bacon, tuna, beef, chicken or tandoori chicken sandwich
- Any bought sandwich containing 350 calories or less – see pages 153–154 in the calorie counter
- Plain omelette + salad/vegetables + glass juice or bowl soup
- 3 crispbread or 3 cream crackers plus one of the following:
  1oz Cheddar cheese
  4oz cottage cheese

individual (40g) portion Camembert/Brie
3 triangles cheese spread
+ mug of soup and piece of fresh fruit
- 1 small pitta bread and 2 tablespoons houmous
- Smoked haddock fillet with 1 slice bread and butter
  + mini fromage frais or diet yoghurt
- Bacon roll – as purchased
- Jacket potato + small portion butter and baked
  beans or coleslaw
  e.g. Spud-U-Like – chilli con carne, hot beans,
  sweetcorn, cottage cheese, tuna salad, prawn cocktail, coleslaw
- Jumbo sausage and baked beans

# MAIN MEAL                                    450 calories

## *Eating at home*

### Home cooking
*Either* – choose one item from each list in any combina-
tion you like. With the meal you may have plenty of
cooked vegetables or undressed salad. To start the meal
you may have a bowl of vegetable soup. Or instead,
have fresh fruit, sugar-free tinned fruit, low fat fromage
frais or diet fruit yoghurt for dessert.

| *List A* | *List B* |
| --- | --- |
| Leg/breast chicken (no skin) | 3 small boiled potatoes (6oz) |
| 3oz roast beef/lamb/pork (cooked weight) | 1 large jacket potato (6oz) |
| 1 ladle stew | 1½oz pasta (raw weight) |

2oz cheese (50g)

6 tablespoons cooked lentils

4oz liver (raw weight)

2 grilled chipolata sausages

Grilled steak (6oz raw)

7–8oz grilled cod/plaice

6 tablespoons cooked beans e.g. kidney

Small grilled lamb or pork chop

4 grilled fish fingers

2 grilled beefburgers

Grilled trout

2 rashers grilled back bacon

2 eggs (not fried)

3 tablespoons boiled rice

½ tin spaghetti in tomato sauce

½ tin baked beans

1½ slice bread + low fat spread

3oz oven chips

6 tablespoons cooked beans

*Or* – any of the special recipe dishes on pages 106–128 with a bowl of vegetable soup to start with, or fresh fruit, sugar-free tinned fruit, diet yoghurt or low fat fromage frais for dessert.

## Chilled or frozen ready meals

*Either* – a chilled or frozen ready meal containing 300 calories or less (see pages 135–137 in the calorie counter) with a large helping of vegetables and one of the following:

2 small boiled potatoes (4oz)

1 medium jacket potato (4oz)

1oz (30g) pasta (raw weight)

2 tablespoons boiled rice

*Or* – any chilled or frozen meal containing 300 to 400 calories (see pages 138–139 in the calorie counter) with a helping of vegetables or undressed salad.

## *Eating out:*

### Restaurant meals – stick to one main course and avoid starters or desserts. The following main courses are suitable:

Poached/grilled fish – avoid eating the sauce if possible

Game – venison/partridge/pheasant/rabbit

Steak – choose the smallest size on offer

Chicken – leg/breast portion not fried

Gammon steak

Plaice in breadcrumbs

Omelette

With the above you may have vegetables or salad and a very small helping of boiled/jacket potatoes.

### Takeaway meals

- Chicken or lamb tikka with salad
- Chicken/beef chow mein or chop suey with 1 to 2 tablespoons boiled rice and Chinese vegetables
- Beef/chicken dish e.g. chicken & mushrooms + 2 tablespoons rice

- Takeaway jacket potato + filling
  e.g. any Spud-U-Like dish except sausage & bean, egg & cheese salad and cheese & onion salad.
- Half of most regular sized pizzas including those from Pizza Hut and Pizzaland both traditional or deep pan
  *or* 1 whole Pizzaland 7" traditional or 5" deep pan pizza except Passionara
- Small doner kebab
- Hamburger or cheeseburger or quarterpound burger including McDonald's hamburger, cheeseburger and quarterpounder. Burger King hamburger, cheeseburger and deluxe cheeseburger. Wimpy hamburger, cheeseburger, kingsize
- Large portion chicken nuggets

# TREATS LIST                **350 calories a week**

You may have two items from both lists once a week.

*List A*
1 glass wine
2 glasses low alcohol wine
½ pint beer or lager
1 pint low alcohol lager
1 pub measure spirits
1 glass sherry
1 large glass fruit juice
1 glass milk
1 individual jam tart
1 fun sized Mars bar/ Snickers

*List B*
1 chocolate digestive biscuit
3 squares milk chocolate
2 boxed chocolates
3 toffees
2 plain biscuits
1 scoop icecream
2 Jaffa cakes
2 crispbread + low fat spread
½oz peanuts
½ bag crisps

1 fun sized Milky Way
1 treat sized Crunchie/
   Wispa
1 treat sized Cadbury's
   Fudge
1 treat sized Double
   Decker

2 pieces fresh fruit
1 banana
1 slice bread
²⁄₃oz cheese

# *Plan 2*

**1,100 calories**

## SNACK MEAL

**300 calories**

You may choose three from the following list daily:
- Medium bowl branflakes or small bowl cornflakes or 2 Weetabix with skimmed milk plus 1 slice toast & scrape low fat spread and one of the following:
  Scrape Marmite or low sugar jam or marmalade
  Piece fresh fruit
  Glass unsweetened apple/orange/grapefruit juice
  Small pot low fat fromage frais/diet yoghurt
  Boiled egg
- 2 slices toast with low fat spread and any of the following:
  2 tablespoons baked beans

2 tablespoons spaghetti in tomato sauce
Boiled or poached egg
1oz Edam or Brie cheese
2oz cottage cheese

- 2 rashers back bacon with a poached egg, grilled tomatoes and half a slice of dry bread or toast
- Fillet smoked haddock or portion boil in the bag fish in sauce *or* 3 grilled fish fingers + one of the following:
  3 small boiled potatoes
  1 large jacket potato
  3oz oven chips
  1½ slices bread & low fat spread
  3 tablespoons spaghetti in tomato sauce
  3 tablespoons baked beans
- 2 grilled pork sausages + 2 tablespoons baked beans or tinned spaghetti
- Plain omelette with one small potato and vegetables or salad
- Lamb chop + one small potato + vegetables
- Shepherd's pie + vegetables
- Hamburger or cheeseburger e.g. McDonald's, Wimpy or Burger King
- Ham, cottage cheese, egg, crab, prawn, salmon or smoked salmon and salad sandwich
- Any sandwich containing 300 calories or less – see list in your calorie counter on pages 152–153.
- 4oz tub cottage cheese + a small roll or 2″ piece French bread or 4 crispbreads and butter. Piece of fruit to follow
- Ham, beef, chicken or prawn salad with a small roll or 2″ piece French bread or 1 4oz jacket potato
- ¼ large pizza or 1 mini pizza + salad
- Jacket potato + cottage cheese or baked beans

- ½ pint vegetable soup with 1 slice bread (dry) or 3 crispbread + 1oz Cheddar cheese
  *Or* 4oz cottage cheese
  *Or* individual (40g) portion Brie/Camembert
  *Or* 3 triangles cheese spread
- Any chilled/frozen diet ready meal

## SMALL SNACK                    50 calories

You may have one from the following list daily:
- Piece fresh fruit (not banana unless small)
- Diet fruit yoghurt
- Low fat plain yoghurt
- Low fat fromage frais
- Glass unsweetened apple/orange/grapefruit juice

## TREATS LIST                    350 calories a week

You may have two items from both lists once a week.

*List A*
1 glass wine
2 glasses low alcohol wine
½ pint beer or lager
1 pint low alcohol lager
1 pub measure spirits
1 glass sherry
1 large glass fruit juice
1 glass milk
1 individual jam tart

*List B*
1 chocolate digestive biscuit
3 squares milk chocolate
2 boxed chocolates
3 toffees
2 plain biscuits
1 scoop icecream
2 Jaffa cakes
2 crispbread + low fat spread

1 fun sized Mars bar/
    Snickers
1 fun sized Milky Way
1 treat sized Crunchie/
    Wispa
1 treat sized Cadbury's
    Fudge
1 treat sized Double
    Decker

½oz peanuts
½ bag crisps
2 pieces fresh fruit
1 banana
1 slice bread
⅔oz cheese

# Case Histories

## Four common problems and their solutions

*Q. Aileen works in a hospital where food is available twenty-four hours a day. As a popular nurse she has the added problem that grateful patients are always giving her boxes of chocolates, or inviting her to share their fruit. Now in her early thirties, she weighs two stone more than she did as a student nurse. Yet she is always busy.*

*A. People who work in hospitals are always faced with such problems. It seems churlish not to take a biscuit when offered. Aileen's best bet is to take one 'for later', just as bar staff do when pressed to have a drink 'for yourself'. If she cannot hold out she should use her treats list and allow herself some of these high calorie foods. As for the open box of chocolates that is a feature of every hospital ward. Well she will just have to walk on past it with her hands in her pockets! Her ideal would be to make it a rule never to eat any extras whilst on duty. In the staff canteen, the best foods to eat are plates of salads or meat and two veg. The choice at night can be very rudi-*

*mentary in some hospitals. Something and chips is often the norm. A sandwich would be a better alternative, or a permitted takeaway once off duty.*

Q. Sandra is a dancer with a big London company. She works late six nights a week, and rehearses four mornings a week. She sleeps in as late as she can and doesn't feel like breakfast before dancing. She has time for a light lunch and a snooze and then she is on stage again. Her main meal is after 11 at night. This is when she is working. On the occasions when there is no show she can choose to eat whatever she likes. It is then she seems to put on weight.

A. Sandra's body must be quite baffled by the different patterns of energy input and output demanded. When she is most energetic she eats least. When she is 'resting' she has time for meals! I can understand why she cannot eat a large meal before she dances. For her, the grazer's diet might have been invented. She should try and eat several nourishing snacks each day. When she is working she doesn't need to be on a strict diet, just eat regularly. When she is resting she should reduce her calorie intake by a third. Eating several small meals is becoming more common these days. It is probably better for you than eating one or two large ones. It all depends on what you choose to eat.

Q. Margaret is a policewoman. She works shifts, but often a job goes on over her hours and she misses a meal. At other times she is nowhere near a café or sandwich bar. She worries that she never seems to eat regular meals and is anxious about the number of chocolate bars and packets of crisps she eats in the pub as her standard fallback snack.

A. Dieting is difficult when you work shifts. Especially if you work nights and bank holidays when everything is closed. If you have no set meal pattern you can end up eating a succession of snacks. If you cannot eat some or all of your meals during conventional hours, think about spreading them over the whole twenty-four-hour period. Your best plan is to try and eat three or four times in eighteen out of those twenty-four hours. Use your diet plan to help you with this. Every week write down the times of your shifts and when you plan to eat something. Stick to the plan even if it means keeping a sandwich in your locker.

Q. Ellen is a teacher who also takes evening classes. By the time she comes home it is too late to shop for her supper. Because she works in the morning as well she can only buy food at the weekend. She ends up living out of the freezer or getting a takeaway. She worries that these meals must be fattening as so many contain pasta or rice, and that she is missing out on fresh vegetables.

A. There is no need to worry if you are not eating home-cooked meals every day. A lot of people don't. In any case takeaway food is usually freshly cooked on the premises and could be better for you than a quick fry-up at home. So long as you make time to cook fresh food on your days off, you can stick to convenience food during working hours. Remember the following though:

a) Avoid takeaway food that has been fried such as fish and chips, sweet and sour pork and onion bhaji. Other takeaway foods are high in hidden fat such as pizza, and are usually too calorific for dieters to eat a whole portion. Chinese food is generally lower in calories than Indian food which often has extra fat, cream or yoghurt in its recipes. Pick a tandoori or tikka (not tikka massala) dish which are dry and lower in calories. You also get a side salad with them. This can take the place of a calorific vegetable curry, unless you have time to make a diet one at home.

b) The rice portion you get from a takeaway is usually far too much for dieters. One portion between two is the rule. Try to cook your own rice at home. 3–4 tablespoons of boiled rice is a suitable amount.

# 5 The Deskbound Diet

This diet allows you 1,000 calories each day. It is the most stringent diet because it has been designed for women who spend much of their working day sitting down. It is suitable for secretaries, computer operators, audio typists, telephonists, receptionists, bank and building society clerks, insurance brokers and light production line work in a factory.

In fact it is for anyone who is anchored to a point of work and therefore has a problem getting enough exercise and using up energy. You could start the day well by walking the last half-mile to work and running up the stairs to your office rather than going by lift or escalator. You could do even more good by walking round the park in your lunch break rather than sitting in a stuffy canteen or eating at your desk.

But the temptations of your work are great. You probably enjoy the company and often go out to a pub or wine bar en masse for lunch. Or perhaps you share a stack of sandwiches dripping with mayonnaise. This is when those fattening sweet biscuits and fizzy drinks get passed around.

So for your diet to succeed, it must take into account that for one meal each day, you will be eating food purchased from outside. This is why you will find we

73

have included takeaways, sandwiches and typical pub and wine bar food in your diet list. They have all been calorie counted and there is a wide selection to choose from. We have also given you a list of treats you can eat each week. This list contains foods such as sweets, chocolates, wine and beer, for the time when it would be rude to refuse a gift from a colleague.

# *Diet Plan* 1,000 calories

## BREAKFAST 150 calories

Choose one of the following:
- 2 Weetabix with skimmed milk
- Medium bowl (50g) All-Bran with skimmed milk
- Small bowl (30g) cornflakes with skimmed milk
- Medium bowl (40g) branflakes with skimmed milk
- Bowl porridge made with 1oz (25g) oats + 150mls milk
- Low fat plain yoghurt + piece fresh fruit & table-spoon muesli or granola
- 1 piece of bread or toast from a large medium sliced

loaf spread with a scrape low fat spread and one of
the following:

Piece fresh fruit (not banana)

Small bowl stewed dried fruit e.g. prunes, apricots

Mini low fat fromage frais

Glass of unsweetened apple, orange or grapefruit
juice

Small (125g) diet fruit yoghurt

Scrape Marmite or low sugar jam or marmalade

Small boiled or poached egg

2 tablespoons baked beans

# SNACK MEAL                          **300 calories**

You may choose any one of these:
- Any standard beefburger in a bun
  e.g. a hamburger from Wimpy, Burger King or
  McDonald's
- Sandwich or small roll with the following fillings:
  cottage cheese, chicken, turkey, ham, crab, smoked
  salmon, prawn, salmon or egg + salad
- Any bought sandwich containing 300 calories or less
  – see pages 152–153 in the calorie counter
- 3" French stick + either 1oz Cheddar cheese
  *Or* Camembert portion
  *Or* 3 triangles cheese spread
- 4oz tub cottage cheese + small roll and piece fruit
- 1 croissant + 2oz cottage cheese + fresh fruit or diet
  yoghurt
- Salad – ham, beef, chicken or prawn + small roll (no
  butter)
- Salad bowl – portion of bean salad, mixed salad and
  pasta or rice salad eaten with a medium jacket potato
  or small roll

- Quarter of a large pizza or 1 mini pizza and salad
- Ploughman's lunch containing the following:
  3" piece French bread, 1oz Cheddar cheese or small wedge Brie, salad, pickled onions, gherkins and red cabbage
- Jacket potato + cottage cheese or coleslaw or baked beans
- Shepherd's pie and veg or salad
- 3 crispbreads spread with 4oz cottage cheese or individual (40g) wedge Brie + a cup or mug of soup or glass fruit juice
- Small bacon roll

# MAIN MEAL                                    **400 calories**

## Home cooking

*Either* – choose one food from list A and one from list B. Have these with a large plate of vegetables or undressed salad. You may either have a bowl of vegetable soup to start, or choose a dessert from one of the following: Fresh fruit, sugar-free tinned fruit, diet fruit yoghurt or a mini low fat fromage frais.

## List A

Leg or breast roast chicken

3oz roast meat

1 ladle stew

4oz liver (raw weight)

4 grilled fish fingers

2 grilled chipolata sausages

4oz grilled salmon

Grilled steak (6oz raw weight)

7–8oz grilled cod or plaice

2oz cheese (50g)

2 eggs (not fried)

6 tablespoons cooked beans e.g. kidney

6 tablespoons cooked lentils

Small grilled lamb or pork chop

2 rashers grilled back bacon

2 grilled beefburgers

Grilled trout

## List B

2 small boiled potatoes (4oz)

2oz oven chips

30g pasta (raw weight)

2 tablespoons boiled rice

1 medium jacket potato (4oz)

¼ packet savoury rice

⅓ tin spaghetti

⅓ tin baked beans

*Or* – one of the special recipe dishes on pages 106–128.

## Chilled and frozen ready meals

*Either* – choose any chilled or frozen ready meal under 300 calories (see pages 135–137 in your calorie counter) with a large helping of veg or salad and piece fresh fruit to follow.

*Or* – any chilled or frozen ready meal between 300 to 400 calories (see pages 138–139 in your calorie counter) with a small helping of vegetables.

## Takeaway food
You may have one of the following:

- Small hamburger or cheeseburger e.g. McDonald's, Burger King or Wimpy
- Jacket potato + coleslaw, baked beans, cottage cheese or prawns
  e.g. Spud-U-Like jacket potato with chilli, hot beans, sweetcorn, coleslaw, cottage cheese, prawn cocktail, tuna salad
- Chicken tikka and salad
- Half of most traditional or deep pan pizzas
  Half of all Pizza Hut deep pan (except Pepperoni Feast) and thin & crispy pizzas, and Pizzaland 10" traditional and 7" deep pan pizzas
  1 whole 7" traditional or 5" deep pan Pizzaland pizza except Passionara

## TREATS LIST                 350 calories a week

You may have two items from both lists once a week.

| *List A* | *List B* |
| --- | --- |
| 1 glass wine | 1 chocolate digestive biscuit |
| 2 glasses low alcohol wine | 3 squares milk chocolate |
| ½ pint beer or lager | 2 boxed chocolates |
| 1 pint low alcohol lager | 3 toffees |
| 1 pub measure spirits | 2 plain biscuits |
| 1 glass sherry | 1 scoop icecream |

1 large glass fruit juice
1 glass milk
1 individual jam tart
1 fun sized Mars bar/
  Snickers
1 fun sized Milky Way
1 treat sized Crunchie/
  Wispa
1 treat sized Cadbury's
  Fudge
1 treat sized Double
  Decker

2 Jaffa cakes
2 crispbread + low fat
  spread
½oz peanuts
½ bag crisps
2 pieces fresh fruit
1 banana
1 slice bread
⅔oz cheese

# Case Histories

## Five common problems and their solutions

*Q. Angela works in a High Street bank, perched on a stool for much of the day. The atmosphere, she says, often gets stuffy behind those reinforced glass windows and the opportunity to get any exercise is virtually nil. Lunchtime is her busiest hour. 'I only have the chance to try and get fit at weekends,' she says. 'And I usually have other things to do.'*

*A. On its own, no exercise will help you lose weight. You need exercise plus diet. But exercise is good for you generally, especially your heart and lungs. The best thing most of us can do is aim for 20 minutes' brisk walking every day. This will help you stay healthy and give your diet a bit of a boost.*

*Get off your bus or train one stop before your normal one each morning and walk the rest of the way. In the evening, get on one stop further down the road and get off at your normal stop. If you drive to work, leave your car half a mile away and walk the rest of the way. You will probably find it easier to park and may even save time! Always use stairs or walk up the escalator.*

*If you can, try to fit in one hour of regular exercise a week, such as swimming, walking, jogging, cycling or playing badminton or squash. Exercise should be relaxing and fun. So forget about buying an exercise bike or rowing machine. Perhaps you could work out all those frustrations tap dancing!*

*Weekend activities such as washing the car or digging the garden are all quite energy intensive. Although you probably want to relax at the weekend, you may find you feel less relaxed having done nothing but sit round all day. How often have you felt more tired after a long lie in? Think of your holidays and how much more walking and swimming you do. It's not just because you are away from your boss for two weeks that you feel more relaxed!*

*Q. Susan works in a solicitor's office. 'There are no facilities for making lunch,' she says. 'And I haven't got time to mess about making sandwiches in the morning. I often have to buy my lunch from a café or sandwich bar. If I am in court there is only time to grab a snack in the nearest pub or wine bar.'*
*A. The great thing about this diet is that you can eat pub food and sandwiches. They have all been calorie counted and there is a wide selection to choose from. Just remember the following rules, especially if you cannot get exactly what is recommended on your diet plan:*
*a) If you are buying a sandwich, always buy one made with two slices of bread, or a small filled roll. Avoid French stick sandwiches which tend to be larger. If you are having one freshly made for you in the deli, ask for no butter or just a scrape. Go for low fat fillings, such as ham, beef, chicken, cottage cheese, plain egg or salmon. Ask them to put in plenty*

*of salad to help bulk out the sandwich and keep it nice and moist. Avoid mayonnaise and salad cream at all times.*

*b) If you are buying a pot of ready made salad, check what dressing has been added to it. Avoid coleslaw, potato salad and Russian salad. Salads containing pasta, rice, nuts, beans or dried fruit will also be quite high in calories.*

*c) If you want soup for lunch, get a low calorie or clear vegetable type. It is not a good idea to have just soup for lunch. Many soups contain quite a lot of calories but little protein or other nourishment, unless they are homemade.*

*d) The best type of meal out is the traditional roast meat and two veg. Avoid roast potatoes or chips and do not add a lot of thick gravy. A plate of salad would also be a good choice, with a small helping of boiled or jacket potato. But make sure no dressing has been added and that the main part of the salad is suitable. Avoid cheese, scotch egg, pâté, smoked mackerel, pork pie or gala pie.*

*Q. Anthea is an audio typist. On Fridays she and the other office staff go to their local pub or wine bar for a snack lunch. She doesn't want to stop doing this . . . it is the one time in the week she really gets to talk to the others.*

*A. Your list of snack meals includes many items that are generally on the menu in pubs or wine bars. Look them up before you go. As you go to the same places regularly, you probably know the counter staff well enough to ask them pertinent questions, like just what IS the salad dressing. Salads look very fresh and healthy, but if they are covered in mayonnaise or an oily dressing they are NOT slimming. The best type to go for are green salad, tomato salad or any salad that looks as if it contains mostly vegetables. Avoid ones containing a lot of sweetcorn, beans, pasta, rice, nuts or fruit.*

*You can eat a Ploughman's but do not open the butter pat.*

Only eat half the cheese portion if it is traditional Cheddar cheese. If there is a lower fat cheese on offer such as Brie or cottage cheese then choose that instead. Avoid sweet pickle, it is high in calories and sugar. You can eat as many pickled onions as you dare . . . just remember you will be working closely with your colleagues all afternoon!

Q. Brenda is senior secretary in a company head office. It is her job to organise birthday cakes or a goodbye drink. But she is trying to lose weight. What should she do?

A. Take a small slice of cake and leave it at the side of your plate. Nobody will notice in the excitement if you do not eat it. Order a white wine and soda (spritzer) at the pub. Put plenty of ice and lemon in and make it last. Remember to count it as one of your treats.

Q. Claire says she gets really bored at work, tied to her desk at the end of a telephone all day. The trolley lady brings round cake and biscuits with the coffee and tea. As if that was not bad enough, the others in the office buy chocolate and offer her some. What can she do?

A. Don't buy a treat or accept one from the others unless it is one allowed on your treats list. Drink a can of low calorie fizzy drink or spring water before the trolley arrives. If you are hungry it will take the edge off your appetite. Leave an apple or orange on your desk. People will be less likely to offer you chocolate when they see you already have a snack. If you do not have any spare calories for that piece of fruit, fear not. One extra apple occasionally will not be the end of the world.

# 6 *The At Home Diet*

Many women spend a lot of time at home, either working from home, looking after children or caring for the sick and elderly. This diet has been designed with that in mind and would be suitable for housewives, freelance workers, writers, artists and pensioners.

The allowance of 1,000 calories a day is based on the fact that many homeworkers do not always get much exercise. You might think that doing the housework is a good way of using up a lot of calories. Well in our mother's or grandmother's day it probably was. Today a lot of the hardest work is done by machines.

Being on a diet at home has its advantages and drawbacks. On the one hand you have complete control over what you eat. Yet food is on tap 24 hours a day. It provides a welcome break from the desk top computer or the ironing. It is easy to nibble continuously.

This is why there are two diet plans in this section. One is for people who prefer to stick to the traditional three meals a day. Perhaps they need to fit in with their family's routine. The other diet plan is a grazer's plan which allows five small snacks daily. This would suit those who live alone and cannot be bothered to cook proper meals, or get through the day unless they have a snack every three hours.

The food allowed on your diet plan takes account of the fact that you are based at home and have the chance to cook and shop. Takeaway or restaurant food is not included in the diet, but chilled and frozen ready meals are.

# Plan 1          1,000 calories

## BREAKFAST          150 calories

Choose one of the following:
- 2 Weetabix with skimmed milk
- Medium bowl (50g) All-Bran with skimmed milk
- Small bowl (30g) cornflakes with skimmed milk
- Medium bowl (40g) branflakes with skimmed milk
- Bowl porridge made with 1oz (25g) oats + 150mls milk
- Low fat plain yoghurt + piece fresh fruit & tablespoon muesli or granola
- 1 piece of bread or toast from a large medium sliced loaf spread with a scrape low fat spread and one of the following:
  Piece fresh fruit (not banana)
  Small bowl stewed dried fruit e.g. prunes, apricots
  Mini low fat fromage frais
  Glass of unsweetened apple, orange or grapefruit juice
  Small (125g) diet fruit yoghurt
  Scrape Marmite or low sugar jam or marmalade
  Small boiled or poached egg
  2 tablespoons baked beans

## SNACK MEAL                    **300 calories**

You may choose any one of these:
- Cottage cheese, cheese spread, ham, turkey, fish paste or egg & salad sandwich made with low fat spread
- 4oz tub cottage cheese and a roll & butter
- 2 slices (2oz) ham + salad with 2 slices bread & low fat spread or 1 jacket potato
- 1½oz cheese with salad and 1 slice bread & low fat spread
- 1oz cheese + 1 hard boiled egg with salad and 1 slice bread & low fat spread
- 2 grilled chipolata sausages or 2 rashers grilled back bacon + 2 tablespoons baked beans or tinned spaghetti
- 1 large jacket potato (6oz) + a teaspoon of low fat spread and the following fillings:
  1oz Cheddar cheese
  4oz cottage cheese
  ½ tin baked beans
- ½ pint vegetable soup + 1 slice bread (dry) *or* 3 crispbread and one of the following:
  1oz Cheddar cheese
  1½oz Brie or Edam
  4oz cottage cheese

- 3 grilled fish fingers or 1 boil in the bag fish in sauce + 2 small boiled potatoes or 1 medium jacket potato (4oz) + a piece of fresh fruit or diet yoghurt
- 1 slice toast + low fat spread + ½ 450g tin baked beans or spaghetti
- 1oz cheese + 1 slice bread as cheese on toast Mug of vegetable soup and a piece of fresh fruit
- Mug of soup followed by poached egg on toast and a banana
- 400g tin ravioli with an undressed salad

## MAIN MEAL                                    **400 calories**

### Home cooking
*Either* − choose one food from list A and one from list B. Have these with a large plate of vegetables or undressed salad. You may either have a bowl of vegetable soup to start, or choose a dessert from one of the following:
Fresh fruit, sugar-free tinned fruit, diet fruit yoghurt or a mini low fat fromage frais.

| *List A* | *List B* |
| --- | --- |
| Leg or breast roast chicken | 2 small boiled potatoes (4oz) |
| 3oz roast meat | 2oz oven chips |
| 1 ladle stew | 30g pasta (raw weight) |
| 4oz liver (raw weight) | 2 tablespoons boiled rice |
| 4 grilled fish fingers | |
| 2 grilled chipolata sausages | 1 medium jacket potato (4oz) |
| 4oz grilled salmon | ¼ packet savoury rice |

Grilled steak (6oz raw weight)

7–8oz grilled cod or plaice

2oz cheese

2 eggs (not fried)

6 tablespoons cooked beans e.g. kidney

6 tablespoons cooked lentils

Small grilled lamb or pork chop

Grilled trout

2 rashers grilled back bacon

2 grilled beefburgers

2 tablespoons tinned spaghetti

2 tablespoons baked beans

*Or* – one of the special recipe dishes in Chapter 4.

## Chilled and frozen ready meals

*Either* – choose any chilled or frozen ready meal under 300 calories (see pages 135–137 in your calorie counter) with a large helping of veg or salad and piece fresh fruit to follow.

*Or* – any chilled or frozen ready meal between 300 to 400 calories (see pages 138–139 in your calorie counter) with a small helping of vegetables.

# TREATS LIST          **350 calories a week**

You may have two items from both lists once a week.

*List A*
1 glass wine
2 glasses low alcohol wine
½ pint beer or lager
1 pint low alcohol lager
1 pub measure spirits
1 glass sherry
1 large glass fruit juice
1 glass milk
1 individual jam tart
1 fun sized Mars bar/ Snickers
1 fun sized Milky Way
1 treat sized Crunchie/ Wispa
1 treat sized Cadbury's Fudge
1 treat sized Double Decker

*List B*
1 chocolate digestive biscuit
3 squares milk chocolate
2 boxed chocolates
3 toffees
2 plain biscuits
1 scoop icecream
2 Jaffa cakes
2 crispbread + low fat spread
½oz peanuts
½ bag crisps
2 pieces fresh fruit
1 banana
1 slice bread
⅔oz cheese

# *Plan 2*                                    **1,000 calories**

## SNACK MEAL                          **200 calories**

You may have four choices from this list daily:
- 1 slice bread/toast + low fat spread and one of the following:
  ¾oz Cheddar cheese
  2oz ham
  1 egg
  4oz tub cottage cheese
  3 triangles cheese spread
  1oz Brie/Edam cheese
  2 sardines
  1 rasher back bacon
  1 grilled chipolata sausage
  3 tablespoons baked beans or tinned spaghetti
- 2 fish fingers or 1 grilled sausage or 1 egg (not fried) with 3 tablespoons baked beans or spaghetti and grilled tomatoes
- Very small grilled lamb chop & vegetables
- 6oz grilled cod or plaice with vegetables
- Boil in the bag fish in sauce + vegetables
- 1 bowl of branflakes or 2 Weetabix with skimmed milk and a diet fruit yoghurt or piece of fresh fruit
- 3oz ham or 4 slices chicken roll or 1 hard boiled egg and salad + 1 slice bread and low fat spread
- ½ pint thick vegetable soup with ½oz grated cheese and 1 slice dry bread
- 2 crispbread + 1oz Cheddar cheese or 1½oz Edam or Brie + a diet fruit yoghurt or piece fresh fruit
- 2oz ham or chicken chopped and added to ⅓ packet savoury rice

- 5oz jacket potato + ¾oz grated cheese or 2 table-spoons baked beans or 4oz cottage cheese

## SMALL SNACK                          **50 calories**

You may have one of the following daily:
- Piece fresh fruit (not banana)
- Portion sugar-free tinned fruit
- Small bowl fresh fruit salad
- Diet fruit yoghurt
- Small pot low fat fromage frais
- Small glass unsweetened apple/orange/grapefruit juice

## TREATS LIST                     **350 calories a week**

You may have two items from both lists once a week.

*List A*
1 glass wine
2 glasses low alcohol wine
½ pint beer or lager
1 pint low alcohol lager
1 pub measure spirits
1 glass sherry
1 large glass fruit juice
1 glass milk
1 individual jam tart
1 fun sized Mars bar/ Snickers
1 fun sized Milky Way

*List B*
1 chocolate digestive biscuit
3 squares milk chocolate
2 boxed chocolates
3 toffees
2 plain biscuits
1 scoop icecream
2 Jaffa cakes
2 crispbread + low fat spread
½oz peanuts
½ bag crisps
2 pieces fresh fruit

90

1 treat sized Crunchie/
  Wispa
1 treat sized Cadbury's
  Fudge
1 treat sized Double
  Decker

1 banana
1 slice bread
⅔oz cheese

# Case Histories

## Five common problems and their solutions

Q. *Janet has tried many diets and never been able to keep to them. Her problem is that she has to cook an evening meal for her family of four. Her husband works in the building trade and can eat more than 2,500 calories a day. Her two teenage sons are also big eaters. She really fancies the full meals they are having and feels miserable making a pathetic salad for herself whilst they enjoy steak and kidney pie. No wonder her resolutions to diet never last for long.*

A. *Don't make life too difficult for yourself by cooking unsuitable food for your family all the time. They can and should be eating healthier food, which would be suitable for you. Try not to give them chips and other fried foods more than once or twice each week. You can eat oven chips once or twice a week anyway, so use those for the whole family. Look up some recipes on pages 106–128. You will see there are all kinds of traditional dishes like beef hot pot and chicken casserole that everyone will enjoy. You simply increase the amounts if you are cooking for your family.*

*The other thing to do is to make sure you have some mouthwatering alternatives in the freezer for the days they do insist on suet pudding. Keep your favourite low calorie frozen meals in the freezer, and eat one of those when the rest of the family have fish and chips. Treat yourself to exotic out-of-season fruits, or a ready-made fruit compote to eat with some low fat fromage frais when they are eating boring old ice-cream.*

Q. *Sally's husband is a long distance commuter. It means that he doesn't get in at night until around 8 p.m., when he is ready for a drink and a snack before he has his evening meal. Sally has tried making their dinner coincide with the time she hears his key in the door, but Mark really needs to sit and relax and talk over his day before he is ready to eat.*

*An added problem is her three children come home in stages from 3.30 p.m. onwards, and they all want their tea before watching a favourite television programme. 'I often end up having two evening meals which is hopeless if I want to stick to a diet,' Sally says. 'I need to see the children get proper food. But it is important to my marriage to share a meal with my husband.'*

A. *You could try eating your main meal with your children one day and your husband the next. On the day you are eating with your husband, have a snack from your treats list or item from your main meal, to eat with your children. On the nights you are eating with your children just eat the starter or dessert course with your husband. There is no need to make either feel left out.*

Q. *Dora lives alone. Like many older people she says she cannot be bothered to cook a proper meal for herself. In any case she finds it difficult to buy meat and vegetables in small enough quantities for one.*

A. *There is nothing wrong with eating mainly snack foods provided you are getting a healthy balance. You get into trouble when the snack is simply tea and biscuits. If you genuinely find life easier by eating snacks go for Plan 2 – the grazer's diet. You can eat several small meals each day and still be within your calorie allocation.*

But do try to include some fresh vegetables in your diet each day. This is not simply an aid to losing weight. Fresh vegetables not only contain fibre but could play a part in preventing major killer diseases such as cancer and heart disease.

Eating alone is a temptation to let things drift and live on tinned food or out of the freezer. It is good to make yourself cook something every couple of days. Perhaps you could invite a friend or neighbour to eat with you once a week. Eating is a very necessary part of our social life and we ignore it at our peril. If this is not convenient, perhaps you can get out to a café or local snack bar. Walking there will do you even more good.


Q. Enid lives on a low income and says she simply cannot afford to diet. 'All the things you must eat on a diet like salads, fresh fruit, fresh meat and fish are all too expensive for me to buy,' she says.
A. Dieting does not have to cost you any more than eating normally. Fresh fruit and vegetables are only really expensive out of season. Study what is in season and buy it when it is cheap. If you cannot afford fresh fish buy frozen fish. Cheap meat is often very fatty. A smaller amount of good quality meat will give better value for money. In any case you will find our menus are full of ordinary foods which should not cost you more than you normally spend. And think what you will be saving on biscuits and chocolate.


Q. Gerrie says she needs help desperately. 'One of the best things about giving up my job to go freelance was the freedom working at home gave me to make cups of tea and coffee whenever I liked. I could work through the lunch hour or stop and eat. Now I find I have put on two stone in six months. This has got to stop.'

A.  It is so easy to drink endless cups of tea and coffee when you are at home. The problem then is that you also get through lots of extra milk. The amount most homeworkers put in their mugs is usually more generous than when you are sharing a carton of milk brought into the office.

On this diet you are allowed six cups of tea or coffee with a little milk. If you want more than this you drink black coffee or lemon tea. Or fill up with low calorie fizzy drinks. Don't hog the fruit juice. Remember how high in calories real fruit juice is and only take it as part of your daily allowance. There is no benefit in cutting down on the amount of liquids you drink. Just drink what you need provided it is low in calories.

# 7 *Life After Your Diet*

By now you will have been following your individual diet plan for just as long as it takes to lose those extra pounds. So far so good, but what happens next?

Every time you come off a diet your body takes some time to adjust to a higher calorie intake. If you go from a low calorie plan straight back to your normal diet you could double your calorie intake overnight. A recipe for disaster!

Everyone wants to eat more food the minute they come off their diet. Food is not only fuel for our bodies, it is an important and enjoyable part of our social life. Despite pressure from all quarters to be slim, we are still expected to eat heartily with family and friends.

Well, as promised, you won't have to alter your way of life. Your diet plan was tailored to suit your life style. So coming off your diet simply means eating more of the same. The answer is to hasten slowly.

# How to increase your calorie intake

Use the meal choices in all four diet plans to help you make the following changes:

**The Travelling Worker** who was allowed **1,200 calories** each day can now increase this to **1,500 calories**. Do this by adding in 3 items from the *extras* list.

**The Odd Hours Worker** who was allowed **1,100 calories** each day can now increase this to **1,400 calories**. Do it by changing your meals like this:

Plan 1, change to:

| | |
|---|---|
| Breakfast | **200 calories** |
| Snack Meal | **350 calories** |
| Main Meal | **500 calories** |

Also add in 2 items from the *extras* list.

Plan 2, keep your meal plan the same but add in to your diet 3 items from the *extras* list.

**The Deskbound Worker** who was allowed **1,000 calories** each day can now increase this to **1,300 calories**. Do this by changing your meals to:

| | |
|---|---|
| Breakfast | **200 calories** |
| Snack Meal | **350 calories** |
| Main Meal | **400 calories** |

Also add in to your diet 2 items from the *extras* list.

**The At Home Worker** was allowed **1,000 calories** each day. Increase this to **1,300** by making the following changes to your meals:

Plan 1:

| | |
|---|---|
| Breakfast | **200 calories** |
| Snack Meal | **300 calories** |
| Main Meal | **450 calories** |

Also add in 2 items from the *extras* list.

Plan 2: keep your meal plan the same but add in 3 items from the *extras* list.

# EXTRAS LIST

⅓ pint milk (semi-skimmed/skimmed) – enough for 6 cups of tea

1 large glass fruit juice

¾oz Cheddar cheese/1oz Brie or Edam/4oz cottage cheese

1 5oz potato

1 banana

2 pieces fresh fruit e.g. apple, orange, pear, peach, nectarine

1 small bowl fruit tinned in natural juice

½ pint vegetable soup

3 crispbread

2 cream crackers

1 slice bread or toast + scrape butter

1 Weetabix/Shredded Wheat + splash milk (skimmed/ semi-skimmed)

1 small bowl porridge made with skimmed milk

1 pot plain yoghurt (low fat or whole milk – not Greek)

1 small pot low fat fruit yoghurt

Continue on your diet and these additional changes for another two weeks.

WEIGH YOURSELF

If you are the same weight within a pound or two as you were when you ended your diet, then you can slowly return to your normal eating pattern.

If you have obviously started to put on weight again,

go back on your original diet for a few days. Check your weight. Now repeat the after-diet diet for another two weeks.

WEIGH YOURSELF AGAIN
You should now be ready to return to a more normal food intake, but there are just a few permanent changes everyone should make.

# *Healthy Eating Plan For Your Life Style*

1. *Eat regularly*. Even if you cannot fit a traditional breakfast, lunch and supper into your life style, always make sure that you eat to a regular plan. Do not go for long periods without food. Try not to eat food late at night, unless it is absolutely necessary. A sensible routine would be:

7–9 a.m. – meal 1 (breakfast)
12–2 p.m. – meal 2 (lunch – snack or main meal)
6–8 p.m. – meal 3 (evening meal – snack or main meal)

2. *Avoid nibbling*. There is nothing wrong with eating small amounts of food frequently, provided it is the right sort of food. High calorie snack foods such as biscuits, nuts, and crisps are not worth the pounds of fat they make you gain. They should be reserved for a weekly treat.

3. *Restrict your intake of high calorie, fatty and sugary foods*. A healthy diet means keeping them to a minimum. But there is no need to avoid them completely. The best

guideline would be to continue to stick to the *Treats List* given at the end of your diet plan. Or take the following advice:

## Chocolate and sweets

Providing your weight is stable, two normal sized chocolate bars *or* two tubes of sweets a week are OK. Look after your teeth and if you must eat sweets between meals, brush your teeth afterwards.

## Biscuits

Be very careful with these. They contain more fat and calories than people realise. It is so easy to have one or two without thinking. Don't buy any biscuits at all, or keep them in the house. If you must buy them, get plain biscuits not digestive, cream or chocolate ones. Whatever kind they are, four biscuits a week should be your absolute limit.

## Cakes and puddings

If you are off your diet, a piece of cake *or* a helping of pudding once a week is acceptable. A slice of plain fruit cake or a scone would be better than a fancy cake, gateau or Danish pastry. If you are having a pudding, choose a milk pudding, fruit and custard or a fruit flan rather than stodgy ones such as bread & butter pudding, sponge or suet puddings. If you eat cakes or puddings once a month or less, throw caution to the winds and eat whatever takes your fancy.

## Icecream

This is a popular item found in most freezers. It is high in sugar and fat. If you want to eat icecream, mousse or other chilled desserts, they should come out of your chocolate ration, or your cake/pudding ration. One helping counts as one bar of chocolate or one portion cake or pudding.

## Yoghurt and fruit

They have probably both featured heavily on your diet. If you want to continue to eat them, then a couple of pieces of fruit daily is fine. If you have had enough of diet yoghurts, remember how calorific all other yoghurts are. If you want to indulge, you should only have one or two pots a week. Stick to diet fruit or low fat plain yoghurts and you can have one every day.

## Fried and fatty foods

Both should still be kept to a minimum. Use these guidelines to keep your fat intake at bay:

- Avoid all fried foods. But if life is unbearable without, allow yourself one item of fried food a week. This should be shallow fried in vegetable oil. A small portion of roast potatoes or oven chips once a week is OK. But remember that although oven chips are lower in fat than ordinary they still contain more than boiled or jacket potatoes. If you want ordinary chips or sauté potatoes, only eat them once a month.
- Try other cooking methods. There are many ways in which you can cook food using little or no fat.

Boiling, baking, microwaving, grilling, stir frying or dry frying using special pans are all suitable. Many foods designed to be fried can easily be grilled or cooked in the oven, e.g. breadcrumbed fish, beef-burgers.

- There are many different types of butter, margarines and low fat spreads. Whatever you use, spread it thinly.

- Milk and cheese are both high in fat. If you like cheese and want to eat it more than 3 or 4 times a week, go for low fat cheeses. Edam, Brie, low fat hard cheese, curd cheese, quark, fromage frais or cottage cheese would all be suitable. If you must drink ordinary milk, do not have more than ⅔ of a pint a day, otherwise try to use semi-skimmed or skimmed milk in tea, coffee and on cereals.

- Crisps, nuts and other savoury snacks should be kept to a minimum. Do not have more than 2 bags a week of any of these snacks.

- High-fat meat dishes should be avoided. For example, sausages are a once-a-fortnight treat.

4. *Watch your alcohol intake.* Like sugar and fat, a healthy diet should not include too much alcohol. Women are more vulnerable to the effects of alcohol than men, and should drink less. Alcohol is also high in calories, as are the mixers you may add. Stick to the Health Education Authority guidelines which suggest 14 units of alcohol a week for women and 21 units for men. A unit of alcohol is ½ pint of beer or lager, 1 glass wine, 1 measure spirits, a small glass of sherry or 1 liqueur. Use only low calorie tonic, lemonade, coke or ginger ale.

Low alcohol or alcohol free wine and lager usually

contain half the calories of ordinary wine and lager. They are not calorie free. Indeed some low alcohol lagers are almost as high in calories as ordinary lager. Strong lagers, or those in which all the sugar has been turned to alcohol, contain more calories than ordinary lager.

5. *If you eat out regularly, still pick and choose your food as carefully as if you were on a diet.*

Restaurants – if you usually eat out more than once a week, limit yourself to a main course and either a starter or dessert. Keep your hand out of the bread basket, and do not use butter. Be wary of starters and desserts. Pâté, pastry, gateau and cheesecake are all loaded with calories. With the main courses, avoid fried foods and cream sauces as a general rule. If you eat out once a fortnight, you can get away with three courses. Still be careful of the obvious high calorie foods. If you only eat out once a month or less then go the whole hog and enjoy it!

Pubs and wine bars – your diet will have taught you which are the best foods to eat in these places. What you do after you finish your diet depends on the frequency of your visits. It is still important to control your alcohol intake and pass on any free nibbles on the bar or at your table. Tapas can be loaded with calories, because a lot of them are fried or served in olive oil. If you are not sure whether any are suitable, avoid them all and choose a main course dish from the menu.

Takeaways – are not necessarily more unhealthy than other foods, but you must be selective. A takeaway should replace a meal, not be eaten as a late evening snack. Make high calorie takeaways such as fish and chips, meat pies and pasties a once-a-month treat.

If you are eating Chinese food go for chop suey, chow mein, chicken or beef dishes and plain boiled rice, rather than sweet and sour dishes, fried rice and spare ribs. When tucking into an Indian meal, avoid massala dishes, or any others with cream or yoghurt sauces. Sometimes the ordinary curry dishes can have a lot of oil in them. Also avoid fried rice, stuffed naan, paratha, fried poppadums and eating a lot of pickles. Go for tandoori, tikka or biryani dishes, plain naan bread or boiled rice.

Most kebabs are OK, but ask for a small one. If you want a burger, avoid the top of the range burgers except for special occasions. French fries should be counted as part of your fried food allowance for the week. Cheeseburgers will always be higher in fat than the standard burger.

Fried chicken should only be an occasional treat. Try to have the chicken with a jacket potato if possible, and avoid coleslaw or potato salad. Pizza and pasta dishes are surprisingly high in calories because of the portion size they give you. They also tend to contain a lot of cheese. Avoid fatty meats on your pizza such as pepperoni or salami.

6.  *Special occasions such as weddings are for you to enjoy, not to worry about what you are eating.* Most people go to one wedding a year if that. So the food you eat on the day will make little difference to your overall intake. Enjoy your food on the day without feeling guilty, or jumping on the scales afterwards.

Christmas is another once a year treat. Food now seems to play a major part in most people's enjoyment of the festive season. Enjoy your turkey, mince pies and Christmas pudding, but do not have large portions. Make sure the special meals and treats last one or two days at the most. Do not overindulge for the whole week. It is usually all the Christmas nibbles that are so damaging to waistlines. Nuts, crisps, mince pies and alcohol are the four you should be most careful of.

7. *Holidays can interfere with your healthy eating life style, but only if you let them.* Holidays are a chance to relax and re-energise ourselves. They are not an excuse for an all-out binge. It can be tempting to load up your plate in the self-service buffet so put plenty of low calorie vegetables or undressed salad on first and leave less room for other things. Avoid fried main courses and keep meat portions small.

Being in the hot sun all day makes you thirsty. Don't drink gallons of fruit juice, have plenty of mineral water or low calorie fizzy drinks instead. Allow yourself an icecream at the beginning, middle and end of your holiday. Watch your alcohol intake, measures of spirits abroad are often twice or three times our own. Finally, get plenty of exercise. Don't just lie on the beach all day. Go swimming, and walk for at least an hour daily.

# 8 *A Month of Recipes*

The following recipes are split into four sections. *Family Favourites* includes good old standbys such as shepherd's pie and chilli con carne. *Quick and Easy* recipes are for those women who do not have the time or inclination after a hard day to spend much time in the kitchen. *Something Different* includes slightly unusual dishes you may want to try as a change from the tried and trusted favourites. Finally the *Special Occasions* recipes are meals you could easily serve up at a dinner party. Why should dieting interfere with your social life?

All the recipes are calculated to provide a total of **800 calories**. This includes any vegetables and potatoes, rice or pasta you may have with them. The quantities for the latter are given in dieter's portion sizes. Every recipe will provide *two reasonable portions*, but naturally if you are cooking for non-slimmers you can allow them more potato, rice or pasta than the quantity given.

# Family Favourites

## COTTAGE PIE

*Ingredients:*
8oz/225g lean minced beef
12oz/350g potato (2 large)
6fl oz/180ml skimmed milk
2 carrots
1 14oz/400g tin tomatoes
4oz/110g mushrooms
1 medium-sized onion
Thyme
Stock

*Method*
Brown the mince in a non-stick pan without added fat.
Put in the diced carrots, sliced mushrooms and diced
onion, and fry gently for 5 minutes. Add the tomatoes,
half a mug of beef stock and the fresh or dried thyme
and simmer for 15 minutes. Meanwhile cook the
potato, and then mash with the skimmed milk. Put the
mince mixture into a fireproof dish and the potato on
top, and brown under a hot grill. Serve with puréed
swede and green beans.

## CAULIFLOWER CHEESE

*Ingredients:*
1 small cauliflower cut into pieces and boiled until
   tender
1oz/30g butter

1 dessertspoon plain flour
2oz/50g grated cheese
Semi-skimmed milk as required
Pepper and salt

*Method*
Melt the butter in a heavy saucepan. Mix in the flour and cook for half a minute. Add grated cheese and seasoning. Thin the roux with a little cold water and add semi-skimmed milk until you have the consistency of a pouring sauce. Drain the cauliflower and place in a serving dish. Pour the sauce over the top. Sprinkle a light coating of fresh breadcrumbs over the top and flash under a hot grill until brown. Serve with a small jacket potato and a tomato and onion side salad.

# MACARONI CHEESE

*Ingredients:*
14fl oz/400ml skimmed milk
4oz/110g strong Cheddar cheese
1 tablespoon cornflour
½ teaspoon English mustard
1oz/30g macaroni per person

*Method*
Add a little of the milk to the cornflour and mix to a

smooth paste. Heat the rest of the milk and add the cornflour mix just before it boils. Stir over a low heat until it thickens, then add in the mustard and most of the grated cheese. Meanwhile cook the macaroni, drain and add to cheese sauce. Sprinkle the remainder of the cheese on the top and brown under the grill. Serve with a crisp green salad.

# SPAGHETTI BOLOGNAISE

*Ingredients:*
8oz/225g lean minced beef
1 14oz/400g tin of tomatoes
1 medium onion
1 clove garlic
1 red pepper
1 stick celery
4oz/110g mushrooms
Oregano or Italian seasoning
1¼oz/35g spaghetti per person
Beef stock

*Method*
Brown mince in a non-stick pan, then add the garlic and onion. Cook gently for 5 minutes and then add the diced pepper and celery. Cook for another 5 minutes, then add the sliced mushrooms and tomatoes. Add half a mug of beef stock and simmer for 20 minutes, adding a pinch of oregano or Italian seasoning. Cook the spaghetti as directed and add to the bolognaise sauce. Add some freshly milled black pepper and serve with a mixed salad. A heaped teaspoonful of Parmesan cheese will add extra flavour and only an extra 20 calories.

# CHILLI CON CARNE

*Ingredients:*
8oz/225g lean minced beef
1 tablespoon red wine
½ 14oz/400g tin kidney beans
1 14oz/400g tin tomatoes
1 medium onion
Pinch chilli powder
1oz/30g rice per person

*Method*
Brown mince in a non-stick pan, and add the sliced onion and cook for a few minutes. Then add the tomatoes, red wine and enough chilli powder to suit your own taste. Cook for 15 to 20 minutes. At the end of cooking add the kidney beans and serve with rice.

# CHICKEN/BEEF CURRY

*Ingredients:*
2 skinless chicken breasts *or* 8oz/225g lean steak
1 14oz/400g tin tomatoes
1 medium onion
1 green pepper
2 cloves garlic
4 cardamom pods crushed
1 fresh green chilli
½ teaspoon coriander
½ teaspoon cumin powder
1 dessertspoon oil
Stock
1½oz/40g rice per person

*Method*

Fry the onions, garlic, pepper and chilli in the oil for 5 minutes. Add the diced chicken or steak and brown well. Sprinkle over the coriander and cumin powder and add the cardamom pods. Cook for another 2 to 3 minutes then add the tomatoes and simmer for 5 minutes. Add enough chicken or beef stock to cover the meat and cook for 20–25 minutes or until cooked. Serve with boiled rice.

# BEEF STEW

*Ingredients:*
8oz/225g lean steak cubed
1 dessertspoon oil
2 carrots cut in chunks
2 onions sliced
1 turnip cut into chunks
1 small leek thickly sliced
2 bay leaves
1 large (6oz) jacket potato per person
Stock

*Method*

Quickly brown the steak in the oil. Add all the vegetables and cook for 5 minutes. Cover with beef stock, put in the 2 bay leaves and cook for an hour in a slow oven, with the jacket potato.

# FISH PIE

*Ingredients:*
6oz/175g smoked cod or haddock
8fl oz/240ml semi-skimmed milk
3 teaspoons cornflour
1 sliced onion
4oz/110g sliced mushrooms
8oz/225g cooked sliced potatoes
Finely chopped fresh parsley
Nutmeg

*Method*
Poach the fish in the milk and then flake it. Poach the onion and mushrooms in the milk and set aside. Mix a little water with the cornflour and make a smooth paste. Bring the milk to the boil and add cornflour mixture. Stir until the mixture thickens. Put the flaked fish, onion and mushrooms into the white sauce. Add a shake of nutmeg and mix in about a dessertspoon of chopped parsley. Cover the fish mixture with the cooked sliced potato. Brush with a little melted butter and brown under the grill. Serve with carrots and cauliflower.

# Quick and Easy

## TUNA PASTA

*Ingredients:*
1 7oz/200g tin tuna fish in brine
1 14oz/400g tin tomatoes
½ medium-sized onion
1 clove garlic
4oz/110g mushrooms
1 dessertspoon oil
Basil (fresh or dried)
6 black olives (optional)
2½oz/50g pasta per person

*Method*
Sweat the finely chopped onion and crushed garlic in the oil in a non-stick pan for 5 minutes. When soft, add the sliced mushrooms and cook for a further 2 to 3 minutes. Add the tomatoes and some fresh or dried basil. Simmer for 10 minutes. Flake the tuna fish and add to the sauce together with the olives. When that has heated through add the cooked pasta and serve with sliced green beans.

## QUICK TUNA MACARONI

*Ingredients:*
1 14oz/400g tin tuna fish in brine
1 10oz/275g tin condensed mushroom soup
1½oz/40g macaroni per person

*Method*

Mix the soup and tuna together in a saucepan, and heat gently for about 10 minutes. Cook the macaroni and add to the tuna pasta mixture and serve with a fresh tomato salad.

# LAMB POCKETS

*Ingredients:*
2 small pitta breads
4oz/110g lamb fillet sliced
1 medium onion
4 medium tomatoes
1 large flat field mushroom
1 red pepper
2 tablespoons low fat plain yoghurt
1 teaspoon cumin
1 teaspoon garam masala

*Method*

Oil a non-stick frying pan and put it on a high heat. Add the pieces of meat and seal them quickly. Cut up the vegetables into small pieces. Turn down the heat and add the onion to the pan and sweat until moist. Add the red pepper and when that begins to soften add the tomatoes and mushroom. Sprinkle on the spices and simmer gently for a few minutes until the lamb is cooked. Turn off the heat and mix in the plain yoghurt. Split open a pitta bread and stuff with this mixture.

# HERB OMELETTE

*Ingredients per person:*
2 size four eggs
1 tablespoon water
½ teaspoon butter
2 teaspoons finely chopped fresh herbs e.g. chives, thyme and tarragon

*Method*
Place the butter in an omelette pan over a medium heat. When it bubbles swirl it around to coat the base. Whisk the eggs, water and herbs together and add to the pan. Cook for 2 minutes, picking up the edges with a spatula so that all the egg is cooked. Flip over and serve at once. With the omelette you may have a 6oz jacket potato or 1 slice of bread and butter, and a tablespoon of peas or sweetcorn. You can vary the filling of the omelette by adding mushrooms poached in water.

# CHICKEN KEBABS

*Ingredients:*
2 skinned chicken breasts
1 medium onion
2 rashers back bacon each snipped into 6 pieces
12 halves of apricots fresh or tinned in natural juice
1oz/30g rice per person

*Method*
Turn the grill on to its highest setting. Skewer pieces of onion, diced chicken, halves of apricots and strips of

bacon together. Put the bacon next to the chicken to help keep it moist. Grill until cooked turning once. Serve on a bed of rice with a salad of lettuce, pepper, cucumber and watercress.

# BEAN AND BACON BAKE

*Ingredients:*
2 rashers smoked back bacon
1 15½oz/440g can baked beans
1 small onion
1 tin chopped tomatoes
1oz/30g pasta shells per person
1 tablespoon Parmesan cheese mixed with 1oz fresh breadcrumbs
Pinch of dried Italian herbs

*Method*
Chop the onion very finely. Cut the bacon up into cubes. Heat a non-stick pan and put the bacon cubes in. Cook gently over a moderate heat for 2 minutes and then add the onion. Stir and cook for another 2 minutes. Add the chopped tomatoes and a pinch of dried herbs and cook for 5 minutes. Add the baked beans and cook until the mixture is piping hot. Mix in the cooked pasta shells and place in an ovenproof dish. If the mixture is a little dry add some extra water and a squirt of tomato purée. Sprinkle the cheese and breadcrumb mixture over the top and brown under the grill. Serve with a mixed salad.

# ITALIAN-STYLE TUNA SALAD

*Ingredients:*
6oz/175g tuna in brine drained and divided into chunks
1 medium onion cut into rings
4oz/110g tinned cannellini beans
2 hard boiled eggs sliced
1 clove garlic crushed
Chopped parsley
1 tablespoon vinegar
1 tablespoon lemon juice
Black pepper

*Method*
Combine all the ingredients, leave for 10 minutes and serve with a tomato or green salad.

# PORTUGUESE COD

*Ingredients:*
2" thick steaks of cod
1 14oz/400g tin tomatoes
1 red pepper
1 medium onion
½pint/275ml dry white wine e.g. vinho verde
Chopped parsley
4oz/110g potato per person

*Method*
Sauté the onion in the white wine until transparent. Add the cod steaks and cook for 2 minutes. Add all the other ingredients and season to taste. Put everything in

a lidded casserole dish and place in a moderate oven (180°C) for 20 minutes. When the fish is falling off the bone remove from the oven and serve with the boiled potatoes and broccoli.

# *Something Different*

## BEEF STIR FRY

*Ingredients:*
8oz/225g lean beef cut into strips
1 tablespoon soy sauce
1 teaspoon Chinese five spice powder
1 teaspoon ground ginger
1 dessertspoon olive oil
2oz/50g beansprouts
2oz/50g water chestnuts
2oz/50g sweetcorn
6 spring onions chopped
1 large carrot cut into matchsticks
1 green pepper cut into strips
1oz/30g rice per person

*Method*
Soak the beef in the oil and spices for 3 hours. Heat a non-stick frying pan or wok, put in the meat mixture and stir fry for 1 minute on a very hot heat. Stir in the vegetables except the beansprouts and turn. Stir in the beansprouts and cook until warmed through and becoming limp. Serve immediately with rice.

# RICOTTA SALAD

For each person place 3oz/75g Ricotta cheese in the centre of a dinner plate. Thinly slice button mushrooms to form a halo around the cheese. Circle this with slices of tangerine or mandarin orange. Surround these by 10 black grapes cut into halves. Peel and slice half a cucumber and arrange this around the grapes. Take a slice of melon, scoop out the seeds and cut the flesh into small half moons. Place these around the edge of the plate. In a small pot shake together the juice of a lemon, a teaspoon of tarragon and half a teaspoon of powdered ginger. Drizzle this mixture over the salad. Serve with a slice of bread and low fat spread or 2 crispbreads and low fat spread.

# CHICKEN AND MUSHROOM AND LEEK PASTA

*Ingredients:*
8oz/225g cooked chicken cubed
6oz/175g mushrooms sliced
1 leek sliced thinly
½oz/15g butter
½oz/15g plain flour
1 clove garlic crushed
1½oz/40g pasta per person
Chicken stock

*Method*
Melt the butter in a heavy pan and fry the leek, garlic and mushrooms until soft. Add the flour and make a roux. Cook for a few seconds and then add enough

chicken stock to make a pouring sauce. Add the cubed chicken and simmer for 5 minutes so that the chicken is properly warmed through. Adjust the seasoning, mix with the cooked pasta and serve with a watercress, cucumber and pepper salad.

# RISOTTO

*Ingredients:*
2oz/50g rice per person
1 dessertspoon oil
8oz/225g chopped ham or 6oz/175g cooked chicken breast
1 carrot diced
1 onion diced
Fresh or puréed garlic
½ red or green pepper
1 tablespoon dry white wine
Fresh thyme

*Method*
Heat the oil in a cast iron casserole. Add the vegetables and a little garlic – fresh or puréed. Stir fry the vegetables for 3 minutes over a moderate heat. Then add the thyme and rice and continue to cook for another 2 minutes stirring constantly. Put in the chopped meat and mix all the ingredients thoroughly. Cover with chicken stock and simmer for 15 minutes. If the mixture becomes too dry, add a little more stock. When the rice is just cooked switch off the heat and add the white wine. Leave for 5 minutes with the lid on and then serve with a mixed salad. Use arborio rice if you can get it, if not basmati rice will do.

# LAMB SQUAB PIE

*Ingredients:*
2 loin lamb chops with the fat removed
1 medium-sized leek, sliced into small rings
1 medium onion cut into quarters
1 eating apple, cored and peeled and sliced into segments
1 teaspoon marjoram
1 teaspoon brown sugar
1 6oz/175g baking potato
1 teaspoon butter

*Method*
Melt the butter in a non-stick pan and seal the chops on both sides. Remove from the pan and place in a high-sided casserole dish. Soften the onion and leek in the buttery pan. Place the apples on top of the meat and add sugar, seasoning and herbs. Cover this with the softened onion and leek. Slice the potato thinly. Put in the frying pan, just cover with water and boil for 5 minutes. Put them over the meat mixture to form a crust. Pour the liquid from the pan into the casserole until it comes to just below the surface. Cook in a hot oven (200°C) for 1 hour and serve with an extra helping of your favourite vegetables.

# CHINESE CHICKEN

*Ingredients:*
8oz/225g raw chicken breast
1 green or red pepper cut into large cubes
2 small courgettes sliced
1 small tin bamboo shoots
½ inch fresh ginger
2 dessertspoons chicken stock
2 dessertspoons dry sherry
1 teaspoon chilli sauce
2 dessertspoons soy sauce
2 teaspoons vinegar
2 teaspoons tomato purée
1 dessertspoon oil
2oz/50g rice per person

*Method*
Cut the raw chicken breasts into 2″ thin strips and marinate in all the liquids except the chicken stock for 10 minutes. Finely chop the fresh ginger. Heat the oil in a wok and stir fry the ginger for half a minute. Drain the chicken reserving the marinade and add to the wok and stir fry for another 1–2 minutes. Put in the vegetables and stir fry for a further minute. Finally add the chicken stock and marinade ingredients. Serve with boiled rice.

# RABBIT STEW

*Ingredients:*
1 joint of rabbit per person
1 medium-sized onion
2 old carrots thinly sliced
8oz/225g tin tomatoes
2 tablespoons peas
Fresh thyme
1 clove garlic
¼ pint/150ml white wine
1 dessertspoon olive oil
2 rashers fat-free back bacon

*Method*
Put the oil in a flameproof casserole and heat on the top
of the stove. Add the rabbit pieces and turn until they
are white. Add the onion and sweat until transparent.
Cut the bacon into strips and add to the casserole dish.
Add the other ingredients and bring to a gentle boil.
Simmer for 1 hour or until the rabbit is tender. Keep it
covered with a lid. Serve with cauliflower.

# CHICKEN AND ASPARAGUS

*Ingredients:*
2 skinless chicken breasts
6 asparagus spears tinned
1 teaspoon butter
Cornflour
4oz/110g potato per person

*Method*

Slice through the length of the chicken just keeping one side as the hinge. Melt the butter in a little water and poach the chicken until cooked, about 10 minutes. Add the asparagus to the pan and warm through. Lift out the chicken and insert 3 asparagus spears into each chicken envelope. Mix a dessertspoon of cornflour, salt and pepper with a little water to make a paste. Pour in a little of the pan juices then return the mixture to the pan adding to the remaining juices. Cook, stirring constantly until the mixture thickens. Serve with potatoes and broccoli.

# Special Occasions

## CHICKEN IN WHITE WINE

*Ingredients:*
2 medium skinless chicken breasts
6fl oz/175ml white wine
1 dessertspoon vegetable oil
4fl oz/110ml chicken stock
Juice of 1 lemon
4oz/110g mushrooms
1 medium-sized onion
Tarragon
2oz/50g rice per person

*Method*

In a heavy based non-stick pan, brown the chicken breast quickly in the hot oil. Add the onion and cook for 5 minutes. Pour in the lemon juice, wine and stock. Put on a tightly fitting lid and simmer for 10 minutes. Now add the finely sliced mushrooms and sprinkle over a teaspoon of tarragon. Cook for another 5 minutes or until the chicken is tender. Remove the chicken and vegetables with a slotted spoon, and reduce the stock until it becomes slightly thickened. Serve the chicken and sauce on a bed of boiled rice with steamed baby carrots and courgettes.

# LIVER IN ORANGE AND DUBONNET

*Ingredients:*

2 thin slices of calves or lambs liver – about 3oz/75g each
1 dessertspoon oil
1 medium-sized onion finely chopped
1 large field mushroom finely chopped
3 sprigs fresh thyme
½ teaspoon butter
¼ pint/150ml fresh orange juice
2 tablespoons Dubonnet
1oz/30g rice per person

*Method*

Heat a heavy based frying pan and put in the oil and butter. Sauté the mushroom and onion plus the thyme. Push to one side and quickly fry the pieces of liver, turning once. Add the orange juice and wine to the pan and warm through. Adjust seasoning and serve on a bed of rice with a green salad.

# BEEF STROGANOFF

*Ingredients:*
8oz/225g fillet steak cubed
1 tablespoon olive oil
4oz/110g mushrooms sliced
1 tablespoon tomato purée
2 Italian tomatoes
1 tablespoon dry sherry
2 tablespoons low fat plain yoghurt
1 medium-sized onion sliced
1oz/30g rice per person

*Method*
Heat the oil in a non-stick frying pan and quickly fry the beef to seal it. Remove from pan and add the onion and mushrooms and sweat together until tender. Stir in the tomato purée, Italian tomatoes sliced and sherry and add seasoning. Put the meat back, cover the pan and cook on a low heat for 5 minutes or until the beef is tender. Add the yoghurt and mix well. Serve with boiled rice and a carrot, orange and tomato salad.

# SOLE WITH GRAPES

*Ingredients:*
2 fillets lemon sole (5oz/150g per person)
20 seedless white grapes
¼ pint/150ml dry white wine
1 teaspoon tarragon
¼ pint/150ml white grape juice
4oz/110g boiled potatoes per person

*Method*
Pour the liquids into an oval dish and lay the fish in flat. Simmer gently on top of the stove until the fish is cooked, turning the sole once. Remove the fish and keep warm. Add grapes, herbs and seasoning to the pan and cook on a low heat for 3 minutes. Serve with boiled potatoes and broccoli.


# SALMON IN A PARCEL

Take a 1″ thick steak of salmon per person. Cut out a piece of foil to make individual parcels. Paint the foil with a little olive oil. Position the steak on the foil. Squeeze the juice of half a lemon over each steak and sprinkle with a little tarragon. Make a julienne of strips of carrot and onion and arrange these on the steak. Season and fold over the foil to make a parcel. Bake in a moderate oven (175°C) for 20 minutes. Serve with 4oz/110g minted new potatoes per person and a mixture of lightly stir fried vegetables including baby corn, mange tout and baby carrots.

# PLAICE IN A LIME SAUCE

*Ingredients:*
4 fillets of plaice (two per person)
1 lime
1 lemon
1 medium-sized carrot
½ pint/275ml dry white wine
1 teaspoon butter
4oz/110g potato per person

*Method*
Melt the butter in a heavy-based frying pan and put in the fish. Sprinkle with the lemon juice and cook slowly. Meanwhile peel the lime and lemon with a potato peeler. Cut the peel into thin strips and add to the pan. Cut the carrot into matchsticks and also add to the pan. Add the wine and cook for a few minutes. Remove the fish and keep warm. Turn up the heat and cook the julienne. Remove from the liquid and serve on top of the fish with new potatoes and whole French beans.

# PRAWN PROVENÇAL

*Ingredients:*
8oz/225g shelled cooked prawns
1 14oz/400g tin chopped tomatoes
1 shallot finely chopped
1 dessertspoon olive oil
1 clove garlic crushed
1 teaspoon basil
1½oz/40g rice per person

*Method*
Warm a heavy-based frying pan and put in the oil.
Sauté the shallot and garlic. Add the tomatoes and
herbs. Simmer for 5 minutes and then add the prawns.
Warm through thoroughly and serve on a bed of rice
accompanied by homemade ratatouille. Make this by
stewing thinly sliced pepper, courgettes and onions
with a tin of chopped tomatoes. A generous measure of
chopped fresh herbs e.g. thyme, basil and oregano will
lift the flavour.

# VEAL ESCALOPES IN CITRUS SAUCE

*Ingredients:*
2 veal escalopes
6 fresh or tinned apricots
1 tablespoon sultanas
¼ pint/150ml orange juice
1 tablespoon sweet sherry or Madeira wine
Olive oil
4oz/110g potatoes mashed with skimmed milk per
  person

*Method*
Paint a frying pan with oil. Put in the veal and quickly
seal each side. Add the other ingredients except potato
and bring almost to the boil. Simmer for 5 minutes, but
not for longer otherwise the meat will go tough. Serve
with mashed potato and fresh peas and carrots.

# 9 *Your Calorie Counter*

This calorie counter lets you know the calorie values of a wide range of foods in their normal portion size. We have done it in this way to make it easier for you to work out your calorie intake, but bear in mind that portion sizes vary a great deal.

## BREAD, ROLLS, CRACKERS, PASTA AND RICE

Add on the following extra calories for butter or margarine:

| Spread on | bread | | toast | | roll | |
|---|---|---|---|---|---|---|
| | *grams* | *calories* | *grams* | *calories* | *grams* | *calories* |
| Butter/hard margarine | 10 | 72 | 12 | 86 | 15 | 108 |
| Soft margarine | 7 | 51 | 9 | 65 | 10 | 72 |
| Low fat spread | 7 | 25 | 9 | 32 | 10 | 35 |

| | | | |
|---|---|---|---|
| Chapati | one made without fat | 50g | 111 calories |
| | one made with fat | 60g | 196 calories |
| Cheese sandwich biscuit | one | 7g | 50 calories |
| Cream cracker | one | 7g | 30 calories |
| Crispbread | one Ryvita type | 10g | 32 calories |
| Croissant | one plain | 50g | 180 calories |

| | | | |
|---|---|---|---|
| | one *pain au chocolat* | 60g | 205 calories |
| Crumpet | one | 40g | 70 calories |
| Dumpling | one suet | 70g | 147 calories |
| Flour | one tablespoon | | |
| | – white | 20g | 69 calories |
| | – wholemeal | 20g | 62 calories |
| French bread | 2″ slice | 40g | 108 calories |
| Fried bread | one slice thick white bread | 48g | 241 calories |
| Malt loaf | one slice | 35g | 86 calories |
| Muffin | one | 70g | 155 calories |
| Naan bread | one | 160g | 376 calories |
| Oatcakes | one | 13g | 57 calories |
| Pasta | average portion boiled | 230g | 268 calories |
| Pitta bread | small | 75g | 198 calories |
| | large | 95g | 251 calories |
| Poppadum | one grilled | 10g | 27 calories |
| | one fried | 13g | 48 calories |
| Pot noodles | as served | 300g | 331 calories |
| Ravioli | average portion | 250g | 174 calories |
| Rice | boiled – brown | 150g | 178 calories |
| | – white | 150g | 184 calories |
| | pilau | 250g | 542 calories |
| | risotto | 300g | 672 calories |
| Rice cake | one | 9g | 28 calories |
| Ritz biscuit | one | 3g | 15 calories |
| Rolls | crusty – white | 50g | 140 calories |
| | – brown | 50g | 127 calories |
| | hamburger bun | 50g | 132 calories |
| | soft rolls – | | |
| | white/brown | 45g | 120 calories |
| | wholemeal roll | 50g | 120 calories |
| Rye bread | one slice | 25g | 54 calories |
| Slimmers' bread | one average slice | 17g | 42 calories |
| Spaghetti in tomato sauce | half a large can | 220g | 129 calories |
| Teacake | one | 60g | 177 calories |
| White bread | sliced | | |
| | – small loaf | 23g | 53 calories |

| | | | |
|---|---|---|---|
| | – large loaf – medium unsliced | 30g | 70 calories |
| | – small loaf | 27g | 66 calories |
| | – large loaf – medium sliced | 35g | 85 calories |
| Wholemeal bread | – small loaf | 25g | 53 calories |
| | – large loaf – medium unsliced | 35g | 75 calories |
| | – small loaf | 30g | 67 calories |
| | – large loaf – medium | 38g | 82 calories |

# BREAKFAST CEREALS

Milk and sugar on cereal adds the following extra calories:

| | | | |
|---|---|---|---|
| Milk – full cream | 64 | Sugar – one level teaspoon | 15 |
| – semi-skimmed | 45 | – one heaped teaspoon | 23 |
| – skimmed | 32 | – one tablespoon | 76 |

| | | | |
|---|---|---|---|
| All-Bran | medium bowl | 50g | 135 calories |
| Bran Flakes (Kellogg's) | medium bowl | 40g | 128 calories |
| Cornflakes (Kellogg's) | medium bowl | 40g | 152 calories |
| Crunchy Nut Cornflakes | medium bowl | 40g | 160 calories |
| Frosties | medium bowl | 40g | 152 calories |
| Fruit 'n Fibre | medium bowl | 40g | 144 calories |
| Grapenuts | medium bowl | 50g | 173 calories |
| Jordan's Original Crunchy | medium bowl | 80g | 282 calories |
| Muesli – | | | |
| Swiss-Style | medium bowl | 70g | 254 calories |
| Extra fruit | medium bowl | 70g | 260 calories |
| No added sugar | medium bowl | 70g | 256 calories |
| Porridge | medium bowl | 180g | 79 calories |
| Puffed Wheat | medium bowl | 40g | 128 calories |
| Ready Brek | medium bowl (raw weight) | 30g | 113 calories |

| | | | |
|---|---|---|---|
| Rice Krispies | medium bowl | 30g | 114 calories |
| Shredded Wheat | 2 bisks | 44g | 145 calories |
| Sugar Puffs | medium bowl | 40g | 129 calories |
| Weetabix | 2 bisks | 40g | 134 calories |

# BISCUITS, BUNS AND PASTRIES

| | | | |
|---|---|---|---|
| Apple strudel | one slice | 115g | 361 calories |
| Baklava (Greek pastry) | one | 100g | 322 calories |
| Bourbon biscuit | one | 12g | 60 calories |
| Brandy snap | one | 15g | 65 calories |
| Chelsea bun | one | 78g | 285 calories |
| Chocolate chip cookie | one | 11g | 50 calories |
| Chocolate eclair | one frozen | 33g | 130 calories |
| | one fresh from bakery | 90g | 335 calories |
| Choux bun | one | 112g | 426 calories |
| Club biscuit | one | 24g | 115 calories |
| Cream horn | one | 60g | 261 calories |
| Currant bun | one | 60g | 177 calories |
| Custard cream biscuit | one | 12g | 61 calories |
| Danish pastry | one medium | 110g | 411 calories |
| Digestive – plain | one McVitie's | 17g | 70 calories |
| – chocolate | one McVitie's | 17g | 73 calories |
| Doughnut | one jam filled | 75g | 252 calories |
| | one ring | 60g | 238 calories |
| | one custard filling | 75g | 268 calories |
| Eccles cake | one | 45g | 213 calories |
| Fig roll biscuit | one | 18g | 60 calories |
| Ginger nut biscuits | one | 9g | 41 calories |
| Harvest Crunch bars | one – average value | 20g | 78 calories |
| Hot cross bun | one | 50g | 155 calories |
| Iced bun | one | 65g | 235 calories |
| Jaffa cake | one | 12g | 43 calories |
| Jam tart | one individual | 24g | 88 calories |
| Jordan's Crunchy bar | one – average value | 33g | 116 calories |
| Lincoln biscuits | one | 10g | 35 calories |
| Macaroons | one | 28g | 124 calories |

| | | | |
|---|---|---|---|
| Malted milk biscuits | one | 9g | 40 calories |
| Marie biscuits | one | 7g | 30 calories |
| Mince pie | one individual | 48g | 203 calories |
| Morning coffee biscuits | one | 4g | 25 calories |
| Nice biscuits | one | 7g | 45 calories |
| Rich tea biscuits | one | 7g | 36 calories |
| Rock cake | one | 45g | 177 calories |
| Scone | one plain | 48g | 173 calories |
| | one fruit | 48g | 151 calories |
| | one cheese | 48g | 174 calories |
| Shortbread | one all butter finger | 15g | 75 calories |
| Teacake | one | 60g | 177 calories |
| Vanilla slice | one | 113g | 372 calories |

# CAKES AND PUDDINGS

| | | | |
|---|---|---|---|
| Apple crumble | average portion | 170g | 336 calories |
| Arctic Roll | one slice | 70g | 140 calories |
| Bakewell tart | one slice | 120g | 547 calories |
| Battenburg cake | average slice | 40g | 148 calories |
| Black Forest gateau | one slice | 90g | 279 calories |
| Bread and butter pudding | one portion | 170g | 272 calories |
| Cheesecake | one slice | 110g | 265 calories |
| Cherry cake | one slice | 42g | 165 calories |
| Chocolate cake with buttercream | one slice homemade | 65g | 296 calories |
| | one slice frozen | 35g | 168 calories |
| Chocolate mini roll | one | 26g | 87 calories |
| Christmas cake | one slice | 70g | 249 calories |
| Christmas pudding | one portion | 100g | 291 calories |
| Crème brûlée | homemade | 109g | 462 calories |
| Crème caramel | shop bought | 90g | 98 calories |
| | homemade | 90g | 152 calories |
| Custard | average portion on pudding | 150g | 176 calories |
| | ready made – half a can | 210g | 199 calories |

| | | | |
|---|---|---|---|
| Custard tart | one individual | 94g | 260 calories |
| Dairy cream sponge | one slice (frozen) | 39g | 123 calories |
| Egg custard | average portion | 140g | 165 calories |
| Fairy cake | one | 28g | 113 calories |
| Fruit cake | one slice plain | 90g | 318 calories |
| Fruit flan (pastry) | one slice | 90g | 106 calories |
| Fruit flan (sponge) | one slice | 90g | 100 calories |
| Fruit pie | average portion | 120g | 442 calories |
| | individual | 50g | 184 calories |
| Fruit sponge | average portion | 170g | 578 calories |
| Gateaux with cream | average slice | 85g | 286 calories |
| Gingerbread | one slice/one man | 50g | 189 calories |
| Icecream | one average slice | | |
| | – dairy | 75g | 145 calories |
| | – non dairy | 75g | 133 calories |
| Instant pudding e.g. | one portion | 120g | 129 calories |
| Angel Delight | | | |
| Jelly | one serving | 200g | 118 calories |
| Lemon meringue pie | one slice | 150g | 484 calories |
| Madeira cake | one slice | 40g | 157 calories |
| Milk puddings | average portion | 200g | 262 calories |
| | small can/ | 215g | 191 calories |
| | half large can | | |
| Mousse – chocolate | one | 60g | 106 calories |
| Mousse – fruit | one | 60g | 82 calories |
| Pancakes | one medium | 110g | 337 calories |
| Pavlova | one portion | 150g | 450 calories |
| Rum baba | one | 198g | 441 calories |
| Sorbet – lemon | one serving | 60g | 78 calories |
| Sponge cake | one slice with | 65g | 318 calories |
| | buttercream | | |
| Sponge pudding with fruit | one serving | 170g | 578 calories |
| Suet pudding | average serving | 150g | 499 calories |
| Swiss roll | one slice | 30g | 82 calories |
| Syrup sponge pudding | one serving | 170g | 562 calories |
| Treacle tart | one slice | 90g | 331 calories |
| Trifle – homemade | one serving | 170g | 272 calories |
| – individual | frozen + cream | 112g | 186 calories |

# CHILLED AND FROZEN READY MEALS

## Under 200 calories

| | | |
|---|---|---|
| **Birds Eye** | | |
| – *Menu Master* | Chicken & mushroom casserole | Liver & onions |
| | Minced beef/vegetables | Shepherd's pie |
| **Findus** | | |
| – *Lean Cuisine* | Turkey in mushroom sauce | Chicken casserole |
| | Cod fillet in tarragon | Plaice Dijonnaise |
| | Fillet of cod mornay | Cod Mediterranean |
| **Marks & Spencer** | Shepherd's pie | |
| **Safeway** | Vegetable chilli | Ratatouille |
| – *Trimrite* | Chicken & mushrooms with vegetables and rice | |
| **J. Sainsbury** | Vegetable dhansak | Roast beef in gravy |
| **Tesco** | Beef Bourguignonne | Broccoli mornay |
| – *Healthy Eating* | Vegetable chilli | Leek & potato bake |
| | Pasta with bolognaise sauce | Sliced roast beef |
| | | Vegetable moussaka |
| **Weight Watchers** | Vegetable chilli | Vegetable hot pot |
| | Vegetable moussaka | |

## 200–250 calories

| | | |
|---|---|---|
| **Boots** – *Shapers* | Moussaka | |
| **Birds Eye** | | |
| – *Menu Master* | Irish stew | |
| **Findus** | | |
| – *Lean Cuisine* | Beef & pork cannelloni | Beef julienne |
| | Chicken & prawn Cantonese | Beef satay |
| | | Zucchini lasagne |
| | Spicy chicken Créole & rice | Moussaka |
| | | Cheese cannelloni |
| | Spaghetti bolognaise | Pasta oriental with |

| | | |
|---|---|---|
| | Cod in white wine sauce | crispy vegetables |
| Marks & Spencer | Sole bonne femme | Salmon paupiettes |
| | Plaice mornay | Cottage pie |
| | Vegetable Cumberland pie | Lamb casserole |
| | | Vegetable curry |
| | Chicken dhansak | Vegetable chilli |
| | Broccoli in cream sauce | |
| Safeway | Vegetable stir fry & beef | Shepherd's pie |
| – *Trimrite* | Spaghetti bolognaise | Roast beef in gravy |
| | Chicken chow mein | Cod Florentine |
| | | Indian style chicken stir fry |
| J. Sainsbury | Chicken do piaza | Cod & prawn pie |
| | Potato & bacon bake | |
| Tesco | Winter vegetable stew & dumplings | Peking sweet & sour |
| | Lancashire hot pot | Vegetable lasagne |
| Waitrose | Tandoori chicken massala | Szechwan prawns |
| | | Chilli & ginger beef |
| Weight Watchers | Chicken korma & rice | Vegetable lasagne |
| | Beef Hungarian & rice | Macaroni cheese |
| | Pasta shells with vegetables & prawns | Cannelloni |
| | | Chow mein |
| | Seafood lasagne | Vegetable au gratin |

## 250–300 *calories*

| | | |
|---|---|---|
| Birds Eye | | |
| – *Menu Master* | Minced beef/veg & mashed potato | Macaroni cheese |
| | Lancashire hot pot | Irish stew |
| Boots | Pasta bolognese | Chicken curry |
| – *Shapers* | Ham & mushroom lasagne | Chicken supreme |
| | | Cannelloni |
| | Tuna & pasta bake | Tagliatelle carbonara |
| Findus | | |
| – *Lean Cuisine* | Lean beef lasagne | Chicken à l'orange |
| | Chicken & oriental | Glazed chicken |

136

|  | vegetables | Sesame chicken |
|---|---|---|
|  | Kashmiri chicken curry | Lasagne verdi |
|  | Lamb tikka massala | Chilli con carne |
|  | Glazed pork Mandalay | Vegetable |
|  | Fisherman's pie with | enchiladas |
|  | broccoli & sweetcorn |  |
| Marks & Spencer | Chicken in tarragon | Chicken bake |
|  | sauce | Chilli con carne |
|  | Beef stew & dumplings | Liver & bacon |
|  | Chicken curry & rice | Plaice Florentine |
|  | Small Cumberland pie | Cauliflower cheese |
|  | Spaghetti bolognaise | Vegetable bake |
|  | Leek & mushroom bake | Vegetable lasagne |
|  | Cabbage & mushroom | Vegetable |
|  | bake | cannelloni |
|  | Vegetable & pasta bake |  |
| Safeway | Chilli con carne | Chicken korma |
|  |  | curry |
| – *Trimrite* | Vegetable lasagne |  |
| J. Sainsbury | Beef stew & dumplings | Cauliflower cheese |
|  | Chicken tikka massala | Chicken & cashews |
|  | Nut cutlets |  |
| Tesco | Cauliflower cheese | Beef hot pot |
|  | crispbake | Chicken chasseur |
|  | Chilli con carne | Vegetable bake |
| – *Healthy Eating* | Pasta with prawns & | Spaghetti |
|  | courgettes | bolognaise |
|  | Chicken casserole & | Ocean pie |
|  | herb dumplings |  |
| Waitrose | Vegetarian shepherd's | Lamb dhansak |
|  | pie | Pork in oyster sauce |
|  | Chilli prawns with rice |  |
| Weight Watchers | Vegetable curry & pilau | Seafood plus |
|  | rice | Sweet & sour + rice |
|  | Chicken marengo & rice | Beef lasagne |
|  | Prawn provençal & rice | Beef oriental + rice |
|  | Seafood mornay & | Tuna cannelloni |
|  | broccoli | Plaice Florentine |
|  | Salmon & prawn |  |
|  | fricasseé |  |
|  | Chicken supreme |  |

## 300–350 calories

| Birds Eye | | |
|---|---|---|
| – *Menu Master* | Seafood & chicken paella | Chicken casserole |
| | The Captain's Pie | |
| – *Healthy Options* | Vegetable lasagne al forno | |
| | Chicken & ham lasagne | |
| Marks & Spencer | Plaice with prawns & mushrooms | Seafood lasagne |
| | Chicken casserole & dumplings | Chicken cordon bleu |
| | Deep filled moussaka | Lasagne |
| | Sweet & sour pork | Linguini & peppers |
| | Chicken tikka massala | Hot & spicy chicken |
| Safeway | Chinese chicken & pineapple | Vegetable lasagne |
| | Chinese style chicken stir fry | Beef Madras curry |
| | | Vegetable rogan josh |
| J. Sainsbury | Tagliatelli + mushrooms & ham | Chicken supreme |
| | Lasagne vegetali | Tagliatelle |
| | Tagliatelli vegetali | Cauliflower cheese |
| | Chicken/oriental vegetable stir fry | Shepherd's pie |
| | Spaghetti bolognaise | |
| – *Healthy Cuisine* | Chicken à l'orange + vegetable rice | Chicken & spinach cannelloni |
| | Filet of beef & green peppers | Pork in oyster sauce + turmeric rice |
| Tesco | Cauliflower cheese | Moussaka |
| – *Healthy Eating* | Chicken supreme with rice | Kashmiri korma |
| Waitrose | Penne arabiata | Vegetable lasagne |
| | Lamb rogan josh | Chicken moghlai |
| | Chicken tikka massala | Shepherd's pie |
| | Chicken chow mein | |

# 350–400 calories

| | | |
|---|---|---|
| Birds Eye | Roast turkey platter | Roast beef platter |
| | Beef stew & dumplings | Spaghetti |
| | Chilli con carne & rice | bolognaise |
| | Beef curry & rice | Lasagne |
| | Prawn curry & rice | Beef goulash |
| | | Fisherman's pie |
| – *Healthy Options* | Vegetable bolognaise | Vegetable tandoori |
| | | curry |
| Findus | | |
| – *Dinner Supreme* | Prawn curry | |
| Marks & Spencer | Salmon à la crème | Seafood linguini |
| | Seafood tagliatelli | Pasta & tuna bake |
| | Steak & vegetable pie | Tagliatelli |
| | Vegetable casserole & | Cannelloni |
| | dumplings | |
| Safeway | Moussaka | Cauliflower cheese |
| | Lasagne | |
| J. Sainsbury | Chicken tikka | Lasagne verdi |
| | Haddock & vegetable | Cannelloni |
| | bake | |
| | Vegetable tikka massala | |
| | Seafood/chicken paella | |
| | stir fry | |
| | Fish lasagne | |
| | Liver & bacon | |
| | Mandalay korma | |
| – *Healthy Cuisine* | Glazed chicken & rice | |
| Tesco | Beef stew & dumplings | Beef stroganoff |
| | Chicken tikka massala | Bombay bhagia |
| | Minced beef & | Kashmiri korma |
| | dumplings | Sweet & sour pork |
| | Tagliatelli carbonara | Beef hot pot |
| | Tuna & pasta salad | Cod & prawn pie |
| Waitrose | Braised steak | Lemon chicken |
| | Tandoori chicken | Beef Madras |
| | massala | Chilli con carne |
| | Cauliflower cheese | Cottage pie |
| | Lamb rogan josh | |

# 400–450 calories

| Birds Eye | Chicken supreme & rice | Cauliflower cheese |
|---|---|---|
| | Chicken curry & rice | Liver & bacon casserole |
| – *Healthy Options* | Tandoori chicken massala | Seafood tagliatelli |
| | Chicken chasseur | Spaghetti bolognaise |
| | Chicken korma | |
| Marks & Spencer | Salmon & herb butter | Chicken Kiev |
| | Chicken korma | |
| Safeway | Macaroni cheese & ham | Cauliflower cheese |
| J. Sainsbury | Chicken & broccoli | Cod & broccoli pie |
| | Lasagne pomodoro | Cannelloni |
| | Chicken Madras & turmeric rice | Toad in the hole |
| | Mushroom & ricotta cheese cannelloni | |
| Tesco | Beef in barbecue sauce | Prawn bhagia |
| | Chicken vindaloo with pilau rice | Lasagne |
| | Chilli con carne with rice | |
| Waitrose | Cannelloni de carne | Lasagne |
| | Sweet & sour chicken with egg fried rice | |

# 450–500 calories

| Birds Eye | Roast chicken platter | Cod mornay |
|---|---|---|
| | Beef rogan josh & pilau rice | Chicken tikka & pilau rice |
| – *Healthy Options* Findus | Chilli con carne | |
| – *Dinner Supreme* | Beef Madras curry | Chicken korma curry |
| Marks & Spencer | Spicy prawns & garlic | Chicken & broccoli pie |

| Safeway | Beef stew & dumplings | Liver & bacon |
| J. Sainsbury | Corned beef hash | Lancashire hot pot |
| | Peking crispy duck | Moussaka |
| | Leek & potato crumble | |
| Tesco | Lamb rogan josh with pilau rice | |
| Waitrose | Penne alla Portofino | Moussaka |
| | Sweet & sour pork with rice | Sausage & mash |
| | | Tagliatelli carbonara |
| | Potato onion & ham bake | Spaghetti bolognaise |

# DRINKS

## *Alcoholic*

| | | | |
|---|---|---|---|
| Babycham | one bottle | 100g | 60 calories |
| Beer | one pint | 574g | 179 calories |
| | one large can | 440g | 137 calories |
| Champagne | one glass | 125g | 94 calories |
| Cider | one pint | 574g | 201 calories |
| Lager | one pint | 574g | 162 calories |
| | one large can | 440g | 124 calories |
| Lager & lime | one pint | 664g | 262 calories |
| Liqueurs | one measure | 25g | 63 calories |
| Low alcohol beer/ lager (average of 4 different brands) | one pint | 574g | 129 calories |
| Martini – dry | one measure | 48g | 75 calories |
| Martini – sweet | one measure | 48g | 80 calories |
| Pils lager | one small bottle | 270g | 105 calories |
| | one large can | 440g | 171 calories |
| Port | one small glass | 50g | 78 calories |
| Sherry | one small glass | 50g | 58 calories |
| Spirits – gin, whisky, | one measure | 23g | 50 calories |

| | | | |
|---|---|---|---|
| rum, vodka, brandy | (England & Wales) | | |
| | one measure (Scotland) | 27g | 59 calories |
| | one airline measure | 48g | 104 calories |
| | one miniature | 29g | 63 calories |
| Stout | one pint | 574g | 207 calories |
| | one large can | 440g | 158 calories |
| Wine | one glass – red | 125g | 84 calories |
| | – white | 125g | 93 calories |
| | one miniature bottle | | |
| | – red | 200g | 135 calories |
| | – white | 200g | 148 calories |
| | one half bottle | | |
| | – red | 375g | 254 calories |
| | – white | 375g | 277 calories |

# FRUIT JUICES AND SOFT DRINKS

| | | | |
|---|---|---|---|
| Apple juice | one glass/small carton | 200g | 72 calories |
| Fizzy apple drink | one glass | 200g | 88 calories |
| Coca cola | one can | 330g | 128 calories |
| Grapefruit juice | one glass/small carton | 200g | 61 calories |
| | one pub bottle | 110g | 33 calories |
| Lemonade | one can | 330g | 69 calories |
| Lucozade | one glass | 200g | 136 calories |
| Mixers | one small bottle tonic/ginger ale | 110g | 22 calories |
| Orange juice | one glass/small carton | 200g | 65 calories |
| | one pub bottle | 110g | 35 calories |
| Pineapple juice | one glass/small carton | 200g | 105 calories |
| | one pub bottle | 110g | 57 calories |
| Ribena | one glass | 200g | 136 calories |
| Squash | one glass | 200g | 42 calories |

| Tomato juice | one glass | 200g | 31 calories |
| | one pub bottle | 110g | 17 calories |
| 'Tropical' fruit juice | one glass/carton | 200g | 90 calories |

# FAST FOOD

This section contains calorie values for the most common takeaway meals. Portion sizes vary and ingredients change, so use the following calorie values as a general guideline only.

## Burgers
*Burger King*

| | | |
|---|---|---|
| Whopper | | 540 calories |
| | with cheese | 613 calories |
| Double Whopper | | 577 calories |
| | with cheese | 829 calories |
| Cheeseburger | | 296 calories |
| | deluxe | 346 calories |
| Double Cheeseburger | | 431 calories |
| | with bacon | 477 calories |
| Hamburger | | 255 calories |
| Chicken royale | | 417 calories |
| Double Barbecue BLT | | 446 calories |
| Crispy Cod | | 394 calories |
| Mushroom Double Swiss | | 426 calories |
| BK Spicy Beanburger | | 516 calories |
| French Fries | – small | 276 calories |
| | – regular | 290 calories |
| | – large | 401 calories |
| Milkshake | (average of 3 flavours) | 312 calories |

*McDonald's*

| | |
|---|---|
| Hamburger | 251 calories |
| Cheeseburger | 295 calories |

| | | |
|---|---|---|
| Quarterpounder | | 415 calories |
| | with cheese | 514 calories |
| Big Mac | | 510 calories |
| Filet-o-Fish | | 361 calories |
| McChicken Sandwich | | 393 calories |
| Chicken McNuggets | (6) | 276 calories |
| | (9) | 415 calories |
| French Fries | – regular | 236 calories |
| | – large | 335 calories |
| Milkshakes | (average of 3 flavours) | 305 calories |

*Wimpy*

| | | |
|---|---|---|
| Hamburger | | 265 calories |
| Cheeseburger | | 305 calories |
| Quarterpounder | | 535 calories |
| | with cheese | 580 calories |
| Kingsize | | 410 calories |
| Halfpounder | | 810 calories |
| Chicken in a bun | | 485 calories |
| Fish & chips | | 445 calories |
| Bacon/Egg in a bun | | 425 calories |
| Bacon in a bun | | 280 calories |
| Spicy beanburger with cheese | | 530 calories |
| Chips | | 265 calories |
| Milkshake | | 255 calories |

# Chinese food

| | | |
|---|---|---|
| Beef dishes | | 345 calories |
| Chicken dishes | | 340 calories |
| Chop suey | | 425 calories |
| Chow mein | | 350 calories |
| Pancake roll | small | 240 calories |
| Prawn crackers | | 260 calories |
| Rice | – boiled | 369 calories |
| | – egg fried | 624 calories |
| Spare ribs in sauce | | 495 calories |
| Sweet and sour pork | | 860 calories |

# Fish and chip shop

| | | |
|---|---|---|
| Chicken portion | one quarter | 409 calories |
| Chips | average portion | 505 calories |
| Fish in batter | average | 377 calories |
| Meat and potato pie | one individual | 784 calories |
| Pastie | medium | 514 calories |
| Rock salmon | average portion | 540 calories |
| Sausage in batter | one | 225 calories |
| Saveloy | one | 170 calories |

# Indian food

| | | |
|---|---|---|
| Chicken curry | | 839 calories |
| Chicken korma | | 735 calories |
| Chicken tandoori | | 721 calories |
| Chicken tikka | | 370 calories |
| Chicken tikka massala | | 501 calories |
| Kebab (Indian) | | 499 calories |
| Meat curry | | 1085 calories |
| Onion bhaji | one | 140 calories |
| Prawn biryani | | 616 calories |
| Samosa | medium – meat | 414 calories |
| | – vegetable | 330 calories |

# Jacket potatoes

*Spud-U-Like*

| | | |
|---|---|---|
| Plain baked potato | | 240 calories |
| | with butter | 325 calories |

Potatoes with hot fillings but no butter:

| | |
|---|---|
| Chilli con carne | 355 calories |
| Hot beans | 320 calories |
| Sausage | 425 calories |
| Sausage & beans | 505 calories |
| Sweetcorn | 340 calories |

Potatoes with salad fillings:

| | |
|---|---|
| Cheese, apple & celery | 485 calories |
| Cheese & onion | 510 calories |
| Coleslaw | 365 calories |

| | | |
|---|---|---|
| Cottage cheese | | 360 calories |
| Cottage cheese & chive | | 360 calories |
| Egg & cheese | | 550 calories |
| Mushroom & rice | | 415 calories |
| Prawn cocktail | | 335 calories |
| Sweetcorn | | 340 calories |
| Sausage salad | | 410 calories |
| Soured cream | | 480 calories |
| Tuna salad | | 340 calories |
| Slimmers Special – cottage cheese with pineapple | | 330 calories |

## Kebabs

| | | |
|---|---|---|
| Doner kebab | – small | 444 calories |
| | – large | 590 calories |
| Shish kebab | meat only | 225 calories |

## Pizzas
*Pizza Hut*

| | Pan Pizza | Thin 'n' crispy |
|---|---|---|
| Cheese Feast | 734 calories | 597 calories |
| Country Feast | 622 calories | 485 calories |
| Hawaiian | 637 calories | 500 calories |
| Margherita | 717 calories | 580 calories |
| Meat Feast | 780 calories | 643 calories |
| Pepperoni Feast | 895 calories | 757 calories |
| Sea Farer | 650 calories | 513 calories |
| Spicy Hot One | 671 calories | 534 calories |
| Supreme | 781 calories | 581 calories |
| Super Supreme | 777 calories | 640 calories |

*Pizzaland*

| Traditional | Seven Inch | Ten Inch |
|---|---|---|
| Caribbean | 368 calories | 649 calories |
| Cheese & Tomato | 328 calories | 569 calories |

| Four Seasons | – | | 720 calories |
|---|---|---|---|
| Hot & Spicy | 371 calories | | 655 calories |
| Passionara | 484 calories | | 869 calories |
| Seafood | 383 calories | | 679 calories |
| Spicy Chicken | 368 calories | | 649 calories |
| Vegetable Special | 344 calories | | 600 calories |

| Deep Pan | Five Inch | Seven Inch | Ten Inch |
|---|---|---|---|
| Caribbean | 398 calories | 701 calories | 1260 calories |
| Cheese & Tomato | 358 calories | 621 calories | 1100 calories |
| Four Seasons | – | 773 calories | 1402 calories |
| Hot & Spicy | 410 calories | 708 calories | 1275 calories |
| Passionara | 510 calories | 921 calories | 1608 calories |
| Seafood | 413 calories | 731 calories | 1323 calories |
| Spicy Chicken | 398 calories | 701 calories | 1261 calories |
| Vegetable Special | 374 calories | 652 calories | 1162 calories |

# FRUIT & VEGETABLES

| Apple | one eating | 100g | 46 calories |
|---|---|---|---|
| | one baked without sugar | 190g | 58 calories |
| Apricot | one raw | 65g | 18 calories |
| Artichoke – globe | one heart | 50g | 7 calories |
| Asparagus | five spears (no butter/dressing) | 125g | 22 calories |
| Aubergine | half cooked without fat | 130g | 18 calories |
| Avocado pear | one half (no dressing/ filling) | 75g | 167 calories |
| Baked beans | one small/half medium can | 225g | 144 calories |
| | one tablespoon | 45g | 30 calories |
| Banana | one medium without skin | 100g | 78 calories |
| Beans – broad | two tablespoons | 120g | 57 calories |
| – french | medium portion | 90g | 6 calories |

| | | | |
|---|---|---|---|
| – kidney | one tablespoon | 30g | 28 calories |
| – runner | medium portion | 90g | 17 calories |
| Beansprouts | one tablespoon | 20g | 2 calories |
| Beetroot | one slice | 10g | 4 calories |
| | one average pickled | 35g | 15 calories |
| Blackberries | one portion (18) | 90g | 26 calories |
| Blackcurrants | stewed no sugar | 140g | 36 calories |
| Broccoli spears | one spear | 45g | 8 calories |
| Brussel sprouts | average serving (9) | 90g | 15 calories |
| Cabbage | medium portion boiled | 90g | 13 calories |
| | one tablespoon pickled | 45g | 6 calories |
| Carrots | medium portion (1 carrot) | 60g | 12 calories |
| Cauliflower | medium portion (9 florets) | 90g | 8 calories |
| Celery | one stick | 30g | 2 calories |
| Cherries | six raw | 60g | 28 calories |
| | one glacé | 5g | 10 calories |
| Chickpeas | one heaped tablespoon | 28g | 40 calories |
| Chinese leaves | one leaf | 40g | 10 calories |
| Coleslaw | one tablespoon | 45g | 36 calories |
| Courgettes | medium portion | 90g | 30 calories |
| Cucumber | average in a salad | 23g | 2 calories |
| | one large pickled | 60g | 7 calories |
| Date | one dried | 15g | 37 calories |
| Fig | one fresh | 55g | 22 calories |
| | one dried | 20g | 42 calories |
| Fruit salad | tinned – average portion | 105g | 99 calories |
| | fresh | 140g | 74 calories |
| Garlic | one clove | 5g | 6 calories |
| Gherkin | one medium pickled | 25g | 3 calories |
| Gooseberries | stewed without sugar | 112g | 15 calories |
| Grapes | small bunch (20 grapes) | | |
| | – white | 100g | 60 calories |
| | – black | 100g | 50 calories |

| | | | |
|---|---|---|---|
| Grapefruit | half raw without sugar | 80g | 17 calories |
| | tinned | | |
| | – in syrup | 105g | 63 calories |
| | – in natural juice | 105g | 46 calories |
| Kiwi fruit | one raw | 60g | 32 calories |
| Leek | one boiled | 160g | 38 calories |
| Lentils | boiled, one tablespoon | 30g | 29 calories |
| Lettuce | average serving in salad | 30g | 3 calories |
| Lychee | one tinned | 13g | 8 calories |
| Mandarin oranges | canned – average serving | 80g | 44 calories |
| Mango | one quarter | 160g | 94 calories |
| Marrow | one third of a marrow | 224g | 14 calories |
| Melon | one slice | | |
| | – canteloupe | 150g | 25 calories |
| | – honeydew | 180g | 37 calories |
| | – watermelon | 200g | 41 calories |
| Mixed vegetables | average portion | 90g | 37 calories |
| Mushrooms | average portion (11) | | |
| | – raw | 60g | 6 calories |
| | – fried | 44g | 92 calories |
| Mustard & cress | quarter of a punnet | 10g | 1 calorie |
| Nectarine | one medium | 150g | 75 calories |
| Okra | average serving (12) boiled | 60g | 10 calories |
| Olive | one | 3g | 3 calories |
| Onion | one average – raw | 90g | 20 calories |
| | – fried | 57g | 196 calories |
| | – pickled | 10g | 2 calories |
| Orange | one medium | 160g | 56 calories |
| Parsnip | one serving boiled | 65g | 36 calories |
| Passion fruit | one | 15g | 5 calories |
| Peach | one medium raw | 110g | 40 calories |
| | one serving tinned | 105g | 91 calories |
| Pear | one conference | 170g | 69 calories |
| | one comice | 250g | 101 calories |

149

| | | | |
|---|---|---|---|
| Peas | one medium portion | 65g | 26 calories |
| Pepper | one half | 80g | 12 calories |
| Pineapple | one large slice – fresh | 80g | 36 calories |
| | two rings – tinned | 80g | 61 calories |
| Plantain | one whole boiled | 200g | 242 calories |
| Plum | one medium | 55g | 20 calories |
| Potatoes | one medium – baked jacket | 180g | 153 calories |
| | average serving | | |
| | – boiled (3) | 180g | 144 calories |
| | – chips (18) | 180g | 454 calories |
| | – croquette (3) | 240g | 90 calories |
| | – mashed (2 scoops) | 120g | 141 calories |
| | – oven chips | 180g | 330 calories |
| | – roast (3–4) | 200g | 314 calories |
| Potato salad | one tablespoon | 45g | 60 calories |
| Prunes | six stewed | 24g | 19 calories |
| Radish | three average | 24g | 3 calories |
| Raisins | one handful (30) | 15g | 36 calories |
| Raspberries | average portion (15) | 60g | 14 calories |
| Ratatouille | one tablespoon tinned | 30g | 22 calories |
| Rhubarb | one serving without sugar (half a pound raw weight) | 150g | 9 calories |
| Spinach | average portion | 90g | 27 calories |
| Spring greens | average serving | 40g | 4 calories |
| Strawberries | ten raw | 120g | 31 calories |
| Sultanas | one handful (30) | 15g | 37 calories |
| Swede | medium serving | 60g | 10 calories |
| Sweetcorn | one tablespoon tinned | 30g | 22 calories |
| | one corn-on-the-cob | 125g | 153 calories |
| Sweet potato | two egg-sized boiled | 130g | 110 calories |
| Tangerine | one medium sized | 70g | 23 calories |
| Tofu | one large cube | 140g | 98 calories |
| Tomato | one medium – raw | 75g | 10 calories |
| | – fried | 69g | 46 calories |
| | average in salad | 34g | 4 calories |
| | tinned – half a tin | 200g | 24 calories |

| | purée – one tablespoon | 15g | 10 calories |
|---|---|---|---|
| Turnip | one whole boiled | 110g | 15 calories |
| Watercress | quarter of a bunch | 20g | 2 calories |
| Yam | boiled – size of medium potato | 130g | 154 calories |

# HOT DRINKS
# All one mug unless otherwise stated

| | | | |
|---|---|---|---|
| Bovril | made with water | 260g | 20 calories |
| Cocoa | made with full cream milk | 260g | 180 calories |
| Coffee | with full cream milk | 260g | 20 calories |
| | black | 260g | 1 calorie |
| Coffee creamer (2 brands) | one teaspoon | 3g | 16 calories |
| Drinking chocolate | made with full cream milk | 260g | 218 calories |
| | made with water | 260g | 64 calories |
| Horlicks | made with full cream milk | 260g | 244 calories |
| Lemon tea | instant | 260g | 35 calories |
| Ovaltine | made with full cream milk | 260g | 241 calories |
| Tea | with full cream milk | 260g | 20 calories |
| | black | 260g | 1 calorie |

# LUNCHTIME SNACKS

Like takeaway meals, lunchtime sandwiches and other snacks vary a great deal in their portion size and amount of fillings.

| | | | |
|---|---|---|---|
| Butter | one wrapped portion | 10g | 72 calories |
| Cheese | Cheddar type – one chunk | 40g | 164 calories |

|  |  |  |  |
|---|---|---|---|
|  | cottage cheese – one tub | 112g | 107 calories |
|  | French Camembert/ Brie | 40g | 122 calories |
| Coleslaw | one tub (8oz) | 224g | 270 calories |
| Croissant | one plain | 50g | 180 calories |
| French bread sandwich | – ham & salad | | 431 calories |
| | – cheese & salad | | 550 calories |
| | – egg & salad | | 430 calories |
| Mixed salad in dressing | one tub | 225g | 76 calories |
| Potato salad | one tub | 225g | 300 calories |
| Sandwiches | typical average homemade or from a deli | | |
| | – cheese & pickle | 138g | 437 calories |
| | – cheese & tomato | 191g | 425 calories |
| | – chicken | 158g | 344 calories |
| | – corned beef | 138g | 360 calories |
| | – cottage cheese | 126g | 280 calories |
| | – egg mayonnaise | 143g | 351 calories |
| | – egg & cress | 130g | 305 calories |
| | – ham | 124g | 286 calories |
| | – roast beef | 138g | 360 calories |
| | – salami | 112g | 398 calories |
| | – salmon | 123g | 301 calories |
| | – tuna | 123g | 351 calories |

# Sandwiches – brand names

## *Under 250 calories*

| Boots – Shapers | Tuna mayonnaise & cucumber |
|---|---|
| | Prawn with egg mayonnaise |
| | Turkey and Chinese leaf with sage & onion |
| | Chicken & grape |
| | Smoked ham, soft cheese & pineapple |

| J. Sainsbury | Red salmon & cucumber |
| Tesco | Healthy eating – beef & salad |
| | Prawn, apple & celery |

## 250–300 calories

| Boots – Shapers | Prawn, apple & celery |
| | Cheese & celery |
| | Chicken & Chinese leaf |
| | Poached Scottish salmon |
| Marks & Spencer | Prawn & cucumber dressing |
| | Salmon & cucumber |
| | Roast beef & salad |
| | Chicken no mayonnaise |
| | Prawn & soft cheese |
| | French vegetable |
| Safeway | Tandoori chicken |
| J. Sainsbury | Chicken & green pepper |
| | Roast beef |
| | Roast beef with horseradish |
| | Scottish smoked salmon |
| | Vegetarian cheddar cheese & spring onion |
| | Red salmon & cucumber |
| | Oak smoked ham, lettuce & tomato |
| Tesco | Ham, cheese & pineapple |
| | Oak smoked ham & salad |
| | Healthy eating – chicken Waldorf |
| | Healthy eating – tuna & cucumber |
| | Healthy eating – prawn cocktail |
| | Roast beef & salad with wholegrain mustard |
| | Smoked salmon with cottage cheese |
| | Roast beef & salad |
| Waitrose | Prawn, mayonnaise & lettuce |
| | Prawn cocktail |
| | Prawn & cheese salad |

# 300–350 calories

| | |
|---|---|
| Marks & Spencer | Smoked salmon |
| | Poached salmon |
| | Medium rare roast beef |
| | Tuna |
| | Egg & cress |
| | Curried coleslaw |
| Safeway | Salmon & cucumber |
| | Chicken & lettuce |
| J. Sainsbury | Corned beef, lettuce & tomato |
| | Ham & tomato |
| | Ham, tomato & coarse grain mustard |
| | Mild cheddar & coleslaw |
| | Free range egg |
| | Smoked ham & chicken |
| | Chicken & coleslaw |
| | Peking duck & hoisin sauce |
| | Tuna & cucumber |
| Tesco | Corned beef & pickle |
| | Free range egg salad |
| | Healthy eating sandwich selection |
| | Prawn mayonnaise (wholemeal) |
| | Roast chicken salad |
| | Prawn cocktail |
| Waitrose | Roast beef, coleslaw & tomato |
| | Club sandwich (turkey & bacon) |
| | Honey roast chicken |
| | Smoked ham & tomato |

# 350–400 calories

| | |
|---|---|
| Marks & Spencer | Prawn with cocktail sauce |
| | Prawn mayonnaise |
| | Prawn & garlic mayonnaise |
| | Poached trout |
| | Ham, mustard & mayonnaise |

|  | |
|---|---|
| | Ham, cheese & coleslaw |
| | Chicken with stuffing |
| | Chicken tikka |
| | Turkey & ham |
| Safeway | Prawn in thousand island dressing |
| | Cheese & tomato |
| | Corned beef & coleslaw |
| | Smoked salmon & cream cheese |
| | Prawn mayonnaise |
| | Red Leicester, spring onion & tomato |
| J. Sainsbury | Chicken salad & mayonnaise |
| | Prawn & mayonnaise |
| | Garlic prawn & mayonnaise |
| | Sausage & egg |
| | Smoked ham & Edam cheese |
| Tesco | Cheese & tomato (wholemeal) |
| | Chinese chicken |
| | Ploughman's sandwich |
| Waitrose | Prawn, mayonnaise & lettuce |
| | Free range egg salad |
| | Egg mayonnaise, salmon & cream cheese |
| | Cheese, mint & cucumber |

## Soup

| | | | |
|---|---|---|---|
| | one sachet made up to one mug | | |
| | average | | 91 calories |
| | average with croutons | | 59 calories |
| | one takeaway serving – average | 170g | 84 calories |
| Vegetable Salad | one tub | 225g | 330 calories |

# MEAT AND FISH

| | | | |
|---|---|---|---|
| Anchovy | one | 3g | 8 calories |
| Bacon – back | one rasher – fried | 25g | 116 calories |
| | – grilled | 25g | 101 calories |
| – streaky | one rasher – fried | 20g | 99 calories |
| | – grilled | 20g | 84 calories |

| | | | |
|---|---|---|---|
| Beefburger | one fried (no bun) | 34g | 89 calories |
| Beef – casserole | medium portion | 330g | 392 calories |
| Beef – roast | medium portion | 120g | 256 calories |
| | one slice | 30g | 64 calories |
| – minced | medium portion | 200g | 260 calories |
| – stew | medium portion | 330g | 392 calories |
| Black pudding | one slice | 30g | 91 calories |
| Chicken – casserole | medium serving | 330g | 313 calories |
| – curry | average portion | 330g | 782 calories |
| – Kiev | average portion | 160g | 390 calories |
| – pie | one slice | 120g | 405 calories |
| – roast | breast | 130g | 184 calories |
| | leg | 90g | 139 calories |
| | drumstick | 47g | 72 calories |
| | medium average portion | 140g | 301 calories |
| Chicken roll | one slice | 19g | 23 calories |
| Chilli con carne | average without rice | 220g | 325 calories |
| Chopped ham and pork | one slice | 14g | 37 calories |
| Cockles | one portion (6–7) | 25g | 12 calories |
| Cod – grilled | one medium fillet | 120g | 113 calories |
| – fried in batter | | 180g | 357 calories |
| Cod in sauce (average of three types of sauce – butter, cheese & parsley) | one portion boil in bag | 170g | 160 calories |
| Corned beef | one thin slice | 30g | 64 calories |
| Cornish pastie | one medium sized | 155g | 514 calories |
| Crab | one small can | 85g | 68 calories |
| Duck | one serving | 185g | 348 calories |
| Eel | one slice | 20g | 40 calories |
| Faggots | two in gravy | 150g | 402 calories |
| Fish cakes | two fried | 100g | 188 calories |
| Fish fingers | two fried | 56g | 130 calories |
| Fish paste | one medium jar | 75g | 124 calories |
| Fish pie | made with potato | 250g | 320 calories |
| Grouse | meat from whole bird | 160g | 276 calories |
| Haddock – smoked | one average fillet | 150g | 151 calories |
| Ham | one average slice | 23g | 27 calories |

| | | | |
|---|---|---|---|
| Heart – lamb's | one cooked whole | 200g | 472 calories |
| Herring | one grilled | 119g | 236 calories |
| | one pickled | 90g | 210 calories |
| Kedgeree | medium serving | 300g | 453 calories |
| Kidney – lamb's | one whole | 90g | 138 calories |
| Kipper | one medium grilled | 125g | 238 calories |
| Lamb – chop | one – meat only | 90g | 199 calories |
| – roast | medium average serving | 120g | 319 calories |
| | one slice | 30g | 79 calories |
| Lasagne | average portion | 450g | 679 calories |
| Lemon sole | one fillet – steamed | 150g | 139 calories |
| Liver – lamb's | one slice fried | 40g | 92 calories |
| – pig's | one slice braised | 50g | 94 calories |
| Lobster | average portion | 85g | 101 calories |
| Luncheon meat | one slice | 14g | 43 calories |
| Mackerel | one whole fried | 220g | 413 calories |
| Moussaka | average portion | 330g | 643 calories |
| Mussels | average portion (5) | 40g | 34 calories |
| Oysters | one | 42g | 34 calories |
| Partridge | meat from one bird | 260g | 551 calories |
| Pâté | for one slice of bread | 40g | 138 calories |
| Pheasant | meat from one bird | 430g | 915 calories |
| Pigeon | meat from one bird | 115g | 264 calories |
| Pilchards | one canned in tomato sauce | 55g | 69 calories |
| Plaice – grilled | one fillet | 130g | 120 calories |
| – fried | | 150g | 341 calories |
| Pork – chop | one chump chop – meat only | 230g | 519 calories |
| – chop | average grilled – meat only | 75g | 169 calories |
| – escalope | one fried | 75g | 169 calories |
| – roast | medium serving | 120g | 343 calories |
| – roast | one slice | 40g | 114 calories |
| Pork pie | one individual | 140g | 526 calories |
| Prawns | average portion (20) | 60g | 62 calories |
| Rabbit | meat from one whole | 510g | 908 calories |
| Ravioli | average serving | 250g | 175 calories |
| Salami | one slice | 17g | 83 calories |

| | | | |
|---|---|---|---|
| Salmon – fresh | one steak – grilled | 100g | 196 calories |
| | one small can | 100g | 154 calories |
| – smoked | average portion | 56g | 79 calories |
| Sardines | average portion tinned (4) | 100g | 217 calories |
| Sausages – beef | one large grilled | 60g | 158 calories |
| | one thin grilled | 35g | 92 calories |
| – pork | one large grilled | 60g | 190 calories |
| | one thin grilled | 35g | 110 calories |
| | one chipolata sausage | 24g | 76 calories |
| | one small hot dog sausage | 23g | 62 calories |
| Sausages and baked beans | small tin | 225g | 276 calories |
| Sausage roll | one medium | 60g | 286 calories |
| Saveloy | one | 65g | 170 calories |
| Scampi | one portion fried in breadcrumbs (10) | 150g | 474 calories |
| Shepherd's pie | average portion | 300g | 356 calories |
| Spaghetti bolognaise | average portion | 450g | 573 calories |
| Squid | one average portion cooked | 65g | 97 calories |
| Steak | medium-sized grilled steak | 115g | 193 calories |
| | large grilled steak | 180g | 300 calories |
| Steak & kidney pie | – individual | 200g | 645 calories |
| | – quarter large tinned | 106g | 342 calories |
| Steak & kidney pudding | individual | 160g | 356 calories |
| Tongue | one slice | 25g | 53 calories |
| Tripe | one portion stewed | 150g | 150 calories |
| Trout | one grilled | 120g | 162 calories |
| Tuna | one small can | 100g | 288 calories |
| Turkey | average portion | 120g | 168 calories |
| Veal | breaded escalope fried | 150g | 322 calories |
| Venison | average portion | 120g | 237 calories |
| Whelks | average portion (4) | 30g | 26 calories |
| Whitebait | average portion fried (20) | 80g | 420 calories |

# MILK, CHEESE, YOGHURT, EGGS, VEGETABLE OILS AND MARGARINE

| | | | |
|---|---|---|---|
| Butter | spread on a slice of bread – medium | 10g | 72 calories |
| | spread on a roll – medium | 15g | 108 calories |
| | one curl | 8g | 57 calories |
| | one portion | 10g | 72 calories |
| | average in jacket potato | 20g | 144 calories |
| Dairy fat spread – margarines containing some butter or dairy fat | spread on a slice of bread | 7g | 46 calories |
| Low fat spread | spread on a slice of bread | 7g | 27 calories |
| Margarine – soft (ordinary & polyunsaturated) | – spread on a slice of bread | 7g | 51 calories |
| Oil – all types e.g. olive, sunflower, corn | one tablespoon | 11g | 97 calories |
| Very low fat spread | spread on a slice of bread | 7g | 19 calories |
| Cauliflower cheese | average portion | 200g | 210 calories |
| Cheese | medium chunk | | |
| | – Brie | 40g | 126 calories |
| | – Caerphilly | 40g | 150 calories |
| | – Camembert | 40g | 118 calories |
| | – Cheddar – full fat | 40g | 164 calories |
| | – low fat | 40g | 104 calories |
| | – Cheshire | 40g | 151 calories |
| | – Danish Blue | 40g | 138 calories |
| | – Double Gloucester | 40g | 162 calories |
| | – Edam | 40g | 132 calories |
| | – Feta | 40g | 100 calories |
| | – Goat | 40g | 78 calories |
| | – Gouda | 40g | 150 calories |
| | – Lancashire | 40g | 149 calories |

| | | | |
|---|---|---|---|
| | – Lymeswold | 40g | 170 calories |
| | – Mozzarella | 40g | 115 calories |
| | – Red Leicester | 40g | 160 calories |
| | – Ricotta | 40g | 57 calories |
| | – Smoked | 40g | 121 calories |
| | – Soya | 40g | 127 calories |
| | – Stilton | 40g | 164 calories |
| | – Vegetarian | 40g | 170 calories |
| | – Wensleydale | 40g | 150 calories |
| Cheese & egg flan | one slice | 120g | 376 calories |
| Cheese sauce | medium portion with main meal | 60g | 118 calories |
| | quarter of a pint | 140g | 277 calories |
| Cheese soufflé | average serving | 110g | 278 calories |
| Cheese spread | one small triangle | 14g | 38 calories |
| Condensed milk | one tablespoon | 25g | 80 calories |
| Cottage cheese | one small tub – plain | 112g | 107 calories |
| Cream cheese | half a small pack | | |
| | – full fat | 30g | 131 calories |
| | – low fat | 30g | 54 calories |
| Cream | one tablespoon | | |
| | – clotted | 30g | 175 calories |
| | – double | 30g | 133 calories |
| | – single | 20g | 42 calories |
| | – sour | 20g | 41 calories |
| | – imitation single | 20g | 39 calories |
| | double | 30g | 94 calories |
| Dried milk | one teaspoon | 3g | 10 calories |
| Egg – duck's | one boiled | 75g | 140 calories |
| Egg – hen's | one boiled (average) | 50g | 73 calories |
| | one fried | 60g | 138 calories |
| | omelette (two eggs) | 120g | 228 calories |
| | one poached | 50g | 77 calories |
| | scrambled (two eggs) | 120g | 295 calories |
| Egg fried rice | average serving | 270g | 561 calories |
| Evaporated milk | one tablespoon | 20g | 31 calories |
| Flavoured milk | one plastic bottle | 500g | 340 calories |
| Fromage frais | small pot | | |
| | – plain | 60g | 67 calories |
| | – fruit | 60g | 78 calories |

| | | | |
|---|---|---:|---:|
| | – very low fat medium pot | 60g | 34 calories |
| | – plain | 100g | 113 calories |
| | – fruit | 100g | 131 calories |
| | – very low fat | 100g | 58 calories |
| Macaroni cheese – homemade | average serving | 300g | 521 calories |
| Macaroni cheese – canned | small can | 210g | 289 calories |
| Milk | half a pint | | |
| | – goat's | 293g | 175 calories |
| | – gold top | 293g | 228 calories |
| | – silver top | 293g | 190 calories |
| | – semi-skimmed | 293g | 134 calories |
| | – sheep's | 293g | 278 calories |
| | – skimmed | 293g | 96 calories |
| | – soya | 293g | 93 calories |
| | – sterilised | 293g | 193 calories |
| | – calcium fortified (average of two) | 293g | 117 calories |
| | average glass | | |
| | – silver top | 200g | 129 calories |
| | – semi-skimmed | 200g | 92 calories |
| | – skimmed | 200g | 65 calories |
| Parmesan cheese | one tablespoon grated | 5g | 20 calories |
| Processed cheese | one slice | 20g | 66 calories |
| Quiche | one medium slice | 120g | 469 calories |
| Scotch egg | one | 120g | 334 calories |
| Welsh rarebit | one slice | 67g | 254 calories |
| Yoghurt | | | |
| – whole milk | small pot – plain | 125g | 98 calories |
| | – fruit | 125g | 131 calories |
| | medium pot – plain | 140g | 110 calories |
| | – fruit | 140g | 147 calories |
| | large pot – plain | 150g | 118 calories |
| | – fruit | 150g | 157 calories |
| – thick & creamy | – fruit | 150g | 153 calories |
| – low fat | small pot – plain | 125g | 70 calories |
| | – fruit | 125g | 112 calories |

| | | | |
|---|---|---|---|
| | medium pot – plain | 140g | 78 calories |
| | – fruit | 140g | 126 calories |
| | large pot – plain | 150g | 84 calories |
| | – fruit | 150g | 135 calories |
| – .diet | small pot – fruit | 125g | 51 calories |
| – Greek | Cow's milk | 224g | 257 calories |
| | Sheep's milk | 224g | 237 calories |
| – soya | medium pot | 140g | 100 calories |
| Yoghurt drink | one small bottle | 200g | 124 calories |

# NIBBLES – CRISPS, SAVOURY SNACKS AND NUTS

## Crisps and savoury snacks
*All values given per bag:*

| | | | |
|---|---|---|---|
| Californian corn chips | | 100g | 570 calories |
| Crisps | – small bag | 30g | 159 calories |
| | – medium bag | 40g | 212 calories |
| Pork scratchings | | 22g | 135 calories |
| Tortilla chips | | 100g | 476 calories |

## Nuts

| | | | |
|---|---|---|---|
| Almonds | six whole | 10g | 56 calories |
| Brazil nuts | three whole | 10g | 61 calories |
| Cashew nuts | one small bag (25) | 25g | 140 calories |
| Chestnuts | five whole peeled | 50g | 85 calories |
| Hazelnuts | ten whole | 10g | 38 calories |
| Mixed nuts & raisins | – small bag | 30g | 133 calories |
| | – medium bag | 40g | 177 calories |
| Peanuts – roasted & salted | – small bag | 25g | 142 calories |
| | – medium bag | 40g | 227 calories |
| Pecan nut | one | 6g | 15 calories |
| Trail mix | one handful | 40g | 198 calories |
| Walnuts | six halves | 20g | 105 calories |

# PARTY FOOD

|  |  | *average values* |
|---|---|---|
| Breadstick | one | 34 calories |
| Crabstick | one | 16 calories |
| Chicken drumstick | one | 72 calories |
| Chicken nuggets | one | 44 calories |
| Carrot stick | half of one whole – raw | 6 calories |
| Celery stick | one | 2 calories |
| Cheese and pineapple on a stick | | 87 calories |
| Dips (various) | large scoop | 115 calories |
| Garlic bread | one 1" piece | 79 calories |
| Garlic mushroom | one | 45 calories |
| Houmous | one scoop (approx one tablespoon) | 80 calories |
| Olives | one | 3 calories |
| Peanuts | one handful (12 whole) | 68 calories |
| Pitta bread | one mini or half one small | 95 calories |
| Pizza | one slice | 175 calories |
| Pork pie (mini) | one | 188 calories |
| Quiche | one small slice | 234 calories |
| Sandwiches | one quarter | |
| | – cheese | 106 calories |
| | – egg/fish/meat | 82 calories |
| Sausage on a stick/ buffet sausage | | 34 calories |
| Sausage roll (mini) | one | 100 calories |
| Scampi | one | 47 calories |
| Taramasalata | average portion | 200 calories |
| Tzatziki (yoghurt & cucumber dip) | large scoop | 48 calories |
| Vol-au-vent | one large | 300 calories |
| | one mini | 90 calories |

# SOUPS, SPREADS AND SAUCES

| | | | |
|---|---|---|---|
| Apple sauce | average portion | 20g | 13 calories |
| Bread sauce | average portion | 45g | 27 calories |
| Brown sauce | one sachet | 30g | 24 calories |
| Bovril | scrape on slice of bread | 1g | 2 calories |
| Cheese sauce | one medium portion | 60g | 118 calories |
| Chutney | one teaspoon | 10g | 15 calories |
| Chocolate spread | average on a slice of bread | 20g | 60 calories |
| Cranberry sauce | average portion | 30g | 42 calories |
| French dressing | average on salad | 15g | 98 calories |
| Gravy | medium serving | 70g | 76 calories |
| Honey | average on a slice of bread | 20g | 57 calories |
| Houmous | one tablespoon | 30g | 80 calories |
| Jam | average on a slice of bread | 15g | 39 calories |
| Lemon curd | average on a slice of bread | 15g | 42 calories |
| Marmalade | average on a slice of bread | 15g | 39 calories |
| Marmite | scrape on a slice of bread | 1g | 2 calories |
| Mayonnaise | average on salad | 30g | 214 calories |
| Mint jelly | average portion | 20g | 52 calories |
| Mint sauce | average portion | 10g | 10 calories |
| Mustard | average portion | 2g | 3 calories |
| Onion sauce | average portion | 60g | 59 calories |
| Peanut butter | average on one slice bread | 16g | 99 calories |
| Pickle | one heaped teaspoon | 15g | 20 calories |
| Prawn cocktail sauce | average | 40g | 114 calories |
| Relish | one teaspoon | 15g | 15 calories |
| Salad cream | average with salad | 30g | 92 calories |
| Soup | average portion | | |
| | – chicken | 220g | 126 calories |
| | – vegetable | 220g | 81 calories |

|  |  |  |  |
|---|---|---|---|
|  | – tomato<br>small tin | 220g | 121 calories |
|  | – chicken | 290g | 168 calories |
|  | – vegetable | 290g | 105 calories |
|  | – tomato | 290g | 159 calories |
|  | packet – made up to<br>half a pint (average of<br>chicken, vegetable &<br>tomato) |  | 116 calories |
|  | with chunks of meat<br>& veg in it |  | 250 calories |
| Soy sauce | one teaspoon | 5g | 4 calories |
| Stock cube | one | 7g | 16 calories |
| Sweet 'n' sour sauce | average | 150g | 95 calories |
| Taramasalata | average portion | 45g | 200 calories |
| Tartare sauce | average serving | 30g | 84 calories |
| Thousand Island<br>dressing | one tablespoon | 30g | 84 calories |
| Tomato ketchup | one sachet | 30g | 28 calories |
| White sauce | with meat/fish/veg –<br>savoury | 60g | 90 calories |
|  | with puddings –<br>sweet | 150g | 257 calories |

# SWEETS, CHOCOLATE, ICECREAM AND SUGAR

|  |  |  |  |
|---|---|---|---|
| After Eight mints | one | 7g | 28 calories |
| Barley sugar | one piece | 7g | 25 calories |
| Boiled sweets | one | 5g | 16 calories |
| Bounty | milk chocolate | 58g | 273 calories |
| Butterscotch | one | 5g | 20 calories |
| Cadbury's Caramel | one | 50g | 245 calories |
| Cadbury's creme egg | one | 40g | 175 calories |
| Chewing gum | one stick | 2g | 10 calories |
| Crunchie | one | 44g | 195 calories |
| Chocolate cream | one | 50g | 210 calories |

| | | | |
|---|---|---|---|
| Chocolate | | | |
| – milk | Aero | 45g | 234 calories |
| | Cadbury's Dairy Milk | 52g | 255 calories |
| | Galaxy | 50g | 259 calories |
| | Yorkie | 70g | 346 calories |
| – plain | Cadbury's Bourneville | 50g | 255 calories |
| nut | Cadbury's Wholenut | 55g | 255 calories |
| | Cadbury's Fruit & Nut | | 230 calories |
| | Yorkie | | |
| | peanut, raisin & biscuit | 70g | 289 calories |
| | honey & almond | 70g | 331 calories |
| | Toblerone – small | 50g | 276 calories |
| Chocolate assortment | Roses/Milk Tray | 8g | 37 calories |
| Choc ice | one average | 48g | 88 calories |
| Cornetto | average | 84g | 219 calories |
| Double Decker | one | 51g | 235 calories |
| Flake | one | 51g | 270 calories |
| Fruit bonbons | one sweet | 7g | 25 calories |
| Fruit gums | five | 10g | 17 calories |
| Fruit pastilles | per tube (12) | 40g | 100 calories |
| Fudge | one square inch | 11g | 45 calories |
| Icecream | one vanilla cornet | | |
| | – dairy | 115g | 223 calories |
| | – non-dairy | 115g | 213 calories |
| | one vanilla tub | | |
| | – dairy | 60g | 116 calories |
| | – non dairy | 60g | 106 calories |
| Ice lolly | average | 75g | 55 calories |
| Jelly babies | one ¼lb box | 115g | 356 calories |
| Kit Kat | four finger bar | 43g | 245 calories |
| Lion bar | one standard | 38g | 258 calories |
| Liquorice allsorts | one ¼lb box | 115g | 391 calories |
| Lollipops | each | 5g | 16 calories |
| Maltesers | each | 2g | 9 calories |
| Mars bar | regular bar | 68g | 293 calories |
| Matchmakers | each | 2g | 9 calories |
| Milky Bar | medium | 20g | 109 calories |

| | | | |
|---|---|---|---|
| Milky Way | standard size | 55g | 236 calories |
| Mints | | | |
| – clear mints | one pack | 39g | 143 calories |
| – strong mints | one pack | 36g | 145 calories |
| – buttermints | each one | 7g | 27 calories |
| – mint imperials | each one | 2g | 7 calories |
| – Polo mints | one tube | 22g | 107 calories |
| Opal Fruits | one tube | 56g | 217 calories |
| Picnic | one bar | | 225 calories |
| Revels | one packet | 40g | 191 calories |
| Rolos | standard tube | | 290 calories |
| Smarties | one tube (36) | 36g | 190 calories |
| Snickers | one bar | 48g | 230 calories |
| Sugar | one level teaspoon | | |
| | – white | 4g | 15 calories |
| | – demerara | 4g | 15 calories |
| | – muscovado | 4g | 15 calories |
| Throat lozenges (Tunes) | one pack | 37g | 136 calories |
| Toffee Crisp | one bar | 40g | 243 calories |
| Tracker | one bar | 40g | 198 calories |
| Treets | one packet | 47g | 247 calories |
| Turkish delight | – chocolate covered bar | 51g | 181 calories |
| | – one square | 15g | 53 calories |
| Twix | one bar | 50g | 239 calories |
| Walnut whip | each one | 37g | 171 calories |
| Wine gums | each one | 3g | 9 calories |
| Wispa | one bar | 41g | 195 calories |

# WINE BAR AND PUB GRUB

| | | *average values* |
|---|---|---|
| Bread | 4″ slice French bread/1 pitta bread/2 slices toast/and one butter pat | 272 calories |

167

| | | |
|---|---|---|
| | – plus one tablespoon taramasalata | 472 calories |
| | – plus one serving pâté | 686 calories |
| | – plus one portion houmous | 352 calories |
| Chilli con carne & rice | | 509 calories |
| Jacket potato | – with butter | 331 calories |
| | – with cheese | 437 calories |
| | – with coleslaw | 223 calories |
| | – with baked beans | 283 calories |
| | – with prawn cocktail | 314 calories |
| Jumbo sausage | – with French bread & butter | 573 calories |
| | – with baked beans | 371 calories |
| Lasagne | | 679 calories |
| Meat pie | | 700 calories |
| Moussaka | | 643 calories |
| Pastie | | 500 calories |
| Pizza | – mini | 200 calories |
| | – medium | 500 calories |
| Plaice & chips | | 795 calories |
| Ploughman's | – with Brie cheese | 477 calories |
| | – with Cheddar cheese | 735 calories |
| | – with pâté | 603 calories |
| Sausage roll (medium) | | 286 calories |
| Scampi & chips | | 928 calories |
| Shepherd's pie | | 356 calories |
| Toasted sandwiches | – cheese & onion/ tomato | 422 calories |
| | – cheese & ham | 341 calories |

## Salads
Main items:

| | | |
|---|---|---|
| Cheddar cheese | (3 thin slices) | 246 calories |
| Cottage cheese | | 107 calories |
| Coronation chicken | | 832 calories |

| | | |
|---|---|---|
| Roast chicken | (breast or leg portion) | 170 calories |
| Roast beef | (3 thin slices) | 192 calories |
| Gala pie | | 475 calories |
| Ham | | 99 calories |
| Peppered mackerel | | 370 calories |
| Pork pie | | 526 calories |
| Prawn cocktail | | 161 calories |
| Quiche | | 469 calories |
| Salmon | | 196 calories |
| Scotch egg | | 334 calories |

| | |
|---|---|
| Portions: | *per tablespoon* |
| Apple, celery & walnut (Waldorf) | 22 calories |
| Bean salad | 60 calories |
| Coleslaw | 9 calories |
| Mixed salad – lettuce, tomato & cucumber | 36 calories |
| Pasta salad | 80 calories |
| Potato salad | 60 calories |
| Rice salad | 100 calories |
| Vegetable salad/ Russian salad in mayonnaise | 66 calories |

# Subject Index

# Recipe Index